I0711427

Explore

The New

YOU

Discover Your Meaning, Build Empowering Habits, Conquer Your Limitations and Lead a Life of Confidence, Abundance and Happiness.

Prabhsimrat Gill

I dedicate this book to my Grand-Parents:

Late Mr. Gian Singh Gill

Late Mrs. Harbhajan Kaur Gill

Late Mr. Bachan Singh Sekhon

Mrs. Mangal Kaur Sekhon

Who all gave me the strength to dream high, fly high, and achieve high and, at the same time, stay humble, grounded, and attached to my roots. Their positivity and blessings have been the driving force that made me feel happy, precious, and joyful! Their teachings and values have played a significant role in my thinking and outlook, helping me shape my life and this book! To express my deepest gratitude for their valuable impact, I dedicate my first work to them and, with that, to my humble and peaceful roots

Contents

INTRODUCTION

If I were to ask you why you picked this book up, what would your answer be? Maybe, you liked the cover, or the title caught your attention. Whatever it is, there was a reason—a meaningful reason—behind your action of paying for this book and starting to read it. There is a reason behind every step you take and every effort you do not wish to make. There is always a reason behind everything that happens in your life. And there is also a reason behind me asking you this question, that is helping you understand the importance of meaning.

One of the deepest desires that almost all of us have is the desire to live a meaningful life. We all wish to leave a significant mark on the world that stays even when we are gone. If you were to ask any person whom you met down the street— "Do you want to live a meaningful life and leave a positive mark on the world?"— the answer will seldom be no, and that is because none of us wants to live a life that has no meaning. And a life without purpose is nothing more than the life of an animal.

However, rarely do all people realize what the meaning in their life is. This is why many people do a particular job because their parents told them to, or study in a specific college just because their friends are there, or are working under a boss and finishing assignments just because the boss told them to. This is the kind of life most common people lead because they do things by following others and merely accepting tasks and orders. If you were to know someone leading a life like this, would you call it a meaningful life? Think about it.

This specific point brings us to the central core of this book— finding meaning and purpose in life to live to the fullest. Being a fourteen-year-old school student and a teenager, I have personally seen many people around me who lead meaning-less lives. I see my schoolmates and many other young, talented people doing things for the sake of someone or something. There are many exam-ples: going to school because it is something that all the people in the modern world do, studying and finishing homework to get good marks, using the good marks to get the latest things, and be-coming a part of the current trends. Whatever these people do isn't governed by their instinct and reasoning, but by society, their parents, and the newest fads. Contrary to the uprising of a video game in my school, I followed my passion by starting a blog and found immense happiness and joy in myself without being on the newest bandwagon. Why so?

When I started on this journey, I had the assurance that I was doing something meaningful and something that I liked! Having that assurance and experiencing it gave me happiness. I was fulfilling my purpose of spreading hope, help, and positivity over the internet through writing, and that feeling of fulfillment gave me innate and real joy! But, when I saw the people around me acting like small, insignificant leaves, aimlessly moving around in a stormy river, it agonized me. Why? Because I noticed that all these people around me did not lead happy lives, even though they were getting almost everything they wanted.

Another human desire that is deep within all our hearts is the desire for happiness. There is not one person on this whole planet who does not want to be happy. However, many people long for joy and wish for it because they don't feel as if they are happy right now. For anyone, there can be multiple, almost unlimited ways to feel happy. You have the choice to watch a light-hearted movie, have a little chat with your friends over a cup of coffee, go on a complete family camping trip, or buy something new that you know is going to make your life easier and happier.

However, something is missing. All these things do make us happy, but only for a temporary amount of time.

A camping trip gives you relaxation and pleasure but doesn't provide you innate happiness that makes you feel good even when you are back in the city. A cup of coffee with friends will allow you some momentary pleasure of socialization. A light-hearted movie will give you brief entertainment and the joy of getting away from your reality, but it won't give you the happiness you seek. You know why? Because there is no meaning to the activities from which you are trying to achieve true satisfaction.

The desire for happiness and the desire for meaning are deeply interlinked, and that is why we cannot achieve happiness without purpose. Happiness is nothing but an inner state where you are entirely calm, relaxed, and satisfied with yourself. And until and unless there is meaning to your life, happiness doesn't come your way.

With this understanding, when I reflect on why many people don't feel pleased even when they have the latest trending watch, the newest phone, the latest clothes, the latest laptop, or the newest anything, the reason doesn't come out to be any physical lack or inadequacy, but the lack of meaning and importance.

When you look at the people around you, you

will realize that most of their mental and emotional suffering rises from a lack of meaning and importance. The reason why inferiority complex develops is that people feel they are not good enough. Anxiety and fear develop because there is uncertainty about the future, which rises when there is no exact meaning to the actions taken. Depression, a significant mental health issue in today's world, arises from the lack of purpose because there is no clarity without meaning. Without clarity, handling problems becomes difficult, and the resulting chaos leads to a confused and chaotic state of mind.

Most of the negative feelings arise from the states of ambiguity, meaninglessness, and lack of importance. It is these three feelings that make people confused, anxious, fearful, and depressed. In the people around me, I saw a lot of fear (especially the fear of missing out), anxiety, aggression, and much more, all of which arise from lack of meaning— resulting in unhappiness.

This inspired me to write this book. I saw that the people around me tried to find and chase happiness in things like the new video game, the new PlayStation, the latest smartphone, and all those things, but they were still unhappy. Whereas I was—to be honest—not even aware of some of the latest things going on in the world of youngsters, but I was still happy. It all boiled down to a sense of optimism, meaning, and importance.

And thus, this book came into being to address the issue most people (not only the youth) face in their lives: unhappiness. A sense of meaninglessness makes people feel unfulfilled in their jobs, relationships, choices, and themselves. This makes people make the wrong career decisions. A person who should have been an engineer is a doctor, and the person who should have been an HR manager is trying to handle a company's accountancy. Everyone has their strengths, and trying to recognize them is the most significant step you take towards fulfillment and purposefulness. If you don't enjoy and don't feel fulfilled with most of the things you do in your day, you cannot be happy, but you can surely change. You have the choice to find meaning in your life and live happily.

In the case of relationships— with friends, parents, colleagues, relatives, or spouses— one of the biggest reasons for conflict and unhappiness is the lack of communication and clarity in what both people expect through the relationship. The lack of clarity arises from ambiguity, confusion, and lack of direction from the inside. If you feel unhappy, you must find meaning in yourself and act on it to develop vision and clarity. You will know what you truly want to do, and when you start to live that, you will be happy. To have happy relationships, you need to be clear on what the basis of your relationships is, and remember, whatever is inside of you goes and reflects outside of you. A happy life filled with happy relationships begins with the rise of satisfaction from within, which happens when you know your purpose and act on it.

So, now is the time to find the answer to the biggest question: should you read this book? Yes! You should, and every person who wants to do something with their lives should read this book. Why? Because in the first section of this book, I provide you with an in-depth breakdown of the process of finding meaning and purpose in life by understanding how you can turn interests into a passion. Then, I move towards the importance of shaping this meaning and purpose into reality by setting the right goals with a proper plan to improve our well-being. After that, we will take a deep dive inside our minds and understand how self-belief and thoughts work, because our beliefs define our world. This section will look at the mindset we need to develop to take the right actions confidently. Finally, in the last section, we will look at how our efforts connect with our minds in the form of habits. We will understand how habits work and how to control them to make it easy to take the right actions with consistency.

If you don't know what to do with your life and feel stuck, this book is for you. If you know what you want but you are unclear on how to proceed and set goals, this book is for you. If you know your passion and purpose, but you don't know how to develop it to the fullest, this book is for you. If you have the skill-set of your passion and know how to set goals, but you are unsure of yourself, this book is for you. If you believe in yourself, have the passion and the goals, but procrastinate and rarely achieve your goals and feel unfulfilled, this book is for you. If you don't face any of these problems and have all the essential knowledge and skills you need to fulfill your meaning, I would still suggest you to read this book, as it is vital to remind yourself of how to navigate through life calmly and happily.

The ways that I teach you in this book are the ones I used to begin writing books, excelling at school, and starting a blog. Through writing, I found my passion, and by turning it into purposeful actions, I found my meaning in life and performing meaningful, and well-directed actions helped me find happiness and joy! You can be rest assured that this is a practical book you can implement in your life! Through this book, I aim to help you find your life's direction, set the right goals, and achieve success. My ultimate reason for writing this book is to help you understand the importance of using your life to the fullest by living meaningfully. And if this book can do that for even one person, my purpose for writing this book is fulfilled! I hope that person is you!

Happy Reading! Enjoy!

Part One

Finding

Meaning

1

The Emergence of Meaning in Your Life

"The meaning of life is not out there but in between our ears. In many ways this makes us the lords of creation."

—*Stephen Hawking*

When you came into being, you were just a small cell, and this is the story of you, from that small cell to the person you are today.

You begin from the fusion of two cells into one. When this happens, you come into existence. You settle down in your mother and start to grow. For the next nine months of your existence, you simply do nothing. Everything is taken care of by your mother, and you continue to enjoy living in your comforting mother. You live through her, and you become one with her.

In this stage, you don't worry about any upcoming math test or what is cooked for lunch today.

You are just enjoying the peace that you have. You don't do anything and you don't think anything. You are just content, happy, and peaceful in this small paradise of yours. For nine months of your existence, you are simply at peace.

However, when you are born after nine months, you lose everything that defined your existence till then. Your connection with your mother, your comforting space, your peace and contentment, your paradise, everything goes away. After birth, you start to look back for that paradise, and that is why you naturally go to your mother. When you are born, you start on a lifelong quest to get your lost paradise back.

You feel the safest around your mother, and that is why you would start crying if a stranger were to hold you. When you are at the infant stage, you still don't know what has happened to you, and that is why you try to find comfort and solace in your surroundings, your father, grandparents, siblings, and other people as they become familiar to you. You also begin to copy and mimic other people's actions and observe things very carefully as a baby because you are always searching for that lost paradise. Whenever something new happens, a glimmer of hope makes you feel that maybe this is how you can achieve the paradise back again.

You continue to grow, learn to walk, learn to speak, and learn to communicate and understand. Now, as you understand the people, the situations, and the things around you, you try to find the same contentment and happiness in that specific thing or action. That is why, as a toddler, you are always curious, asking questions about almost everything!

Then comes the stage of childhood and the age of going to school. During this time, you understand the world pretty well and start socializing with people outside your family. The first day of school is daunting, and the thought of being left alone amid some strangers without your mother and father is terrifying, but you soon adjust to it and try to find joy and happiness here as well. You are always searching for the comfort and the solace of the first nine months of your existence.

Next comes the stage of teenage and philosophical understanding of life. Through multiple activities, books, people, and things, you subconsciously try to find happiness and comfort. You start taking other people's opinions seriously, and in the search for the lost paradise, a sense of insecurity develops. This insecurity kicks off in childhood and builds up in the teenage. Often, there are multiple layers above this sense of insecurity, but the main root of insecurity is not finding peace and happiness.

As your mind soaks in more and more information from the things around you, you start to think about various ways to find the happiness and the mental, physical and spiritual peace you seek. You continue to look outward for the same joy and ease, seeking it in people, activities, and things.

You go through college and you start your own life. Now you feel that you will be happy with your own house, job, friends, life partner, and kids. All of these things make you feel satisfied and content for moments, but without knowing, you still long for the comfort, peace, and happiness of your nine months of paradise. Without the paradise, you internally feel fearful, insecure, and unstable at times. You always have a smile on your face, and you try to find happiness—the real, innate joy—but you rarely find it. You continue to live this way, trying to find peace and happiness, until life passes away.

This seems like a sad story, doesn't it? However, the truth is that most of us are actually in the search for the paradise and the comfort of our mother's womb, whose memories we don't have. We continue to look for the paradise and happiness in our lives through the things, the people, and the actions we take in our life, but we rarely seem to find it.

You may be wondering, is it then wrong to seek and work for happiness and peace when we can't genuinely achieve these states no matter what? Well, the answer to this is no. It is not wrong to seek to live in peace, happiness, and contentment. We can achieve happiness and joy in life; even being at peace with everything is possible. But the reason why all of the happiness, peace, and contentment does not come in most of our lives is that we seek them from the wrong things.

We cannot find peace, contentment, happiness, love, respect, importance, comfort, fearlessness, and much more on the outside, but we can undoubtedly discover them within us. These traits are not found by possessing material things, having a particular job, being with a certain number of people, getting the latest tech gear, or anything else. Happiness, peace, and contentment are right inside you— you just need to look the right way.

Looking inside doesn't mean cutting yourself open and looking at all the systems and organs inside of you! (I am sure none of you would do that!) Looking inside means understanding yourself and finding out who you truly are.

You may be wondering, if we can find happiness, peace, and contentment in the now, then why do we need to have a meaning and strive towards it? Well, it is a logical question, and there is an answer as well! We need to have a purpose in life because we won't have anything to live for without it, except for what an animal does. Yes, we can find happiness and peace in this moment if we want to, but without any meaning in life, we won't feel happy for long. We can take a break, relax, and be joyful in the moment, but without any meaning in life, the happiness won't stick.

In the introduction, we saw why most of my friends and people around me were unhappy; it all boiled down to a lack of sense of meaning and importance. Why so? Because without knowing the meaning in your life, you are like the sole survivor of a wrecked ship wandering about in the sea, with no means or reasons for living. You can find true happiness with meaning, and meaning is found by connecting with yourself. When you connect with yourself and find happiness, you get the peace and the soothing comfort of the first nine months of your existence simply because you now know that you have a meaningful presence.

Various successful people across the world are an exemplary example of this. Some of the happiest and successful people (not only in monetary terms) have found their happiness, contentment, and peace, not by collecting things and earning financial wealth, but by connecting with their meaning and finding their way in life.

This is how meaning emerges in your life, and you can find it by connecting with yourself. It would be best if you find purpose and a reason to live because only then will you be happy and cherish every moment.

2

The Power of Meaning

It was one o'clock at night when thieves raided the train. The passengers in the general compartment hastily handed over their belongings and jewelry out of utter fear and panic as the Padmavati Express made its way from Lucknow to Delhi through some desolate villages and towns. The thieves filled their bags and continued across the train, when one young twenty-two-year-old athlete refused to hand over the gold chain her mom gifted her. The thieves forced her to do so, but she did not budge. The thieves were agitated, but she was stubborn and ready to fight for what was hers by right. The thieves could not tolerate her resistance, and within a few minutes, threw her out of the moving train.

She fell on the tracks as another train approached. She mustered all of her energy and tried to get up and off the tracks. But, too late. Before she could get up, the approaching train crushed her left leg entirely and broke her right leg. She lay there in vain on the tracks in the middle of the night. Her upper right leg had moved below her knees and hung in her jeans as the wounds bled incessantly. In the wee hours of the night, no one came to help her around, no matter how much she cried for help. Her consciousness was ever awake as she counted 49 trains pass over the tracks she was on.

She could not move. One of her arms held her broken right leg while the other arm was broken as well. For over six hours, there was no help. In the morning, some villagers spotted and took her to the local Civil Hospital in Bareilly, a town in the state of Uttar Pradesh in India. Her pain grew ever excruciating as she lay down in the hospital, and doctors discussed hopelessly in a dilemma.

This accident severely crushed her left leg, which had to be amputated to ensure her survival. The doctors did not know how to do that because there was no blood, no anesthesia, and no oxygen available in the hospital. The doctors did not know how to operate and perform the surgery until she spoke out for herself.

She told the doctors to perform the surgery without anesthesia. The doctors, the pharmacists, and almost everyone in the panel was shocked. Who was this brave soul? You may be wondering. This brave soul was a National Level Volleyball Player, Arunima Sinha, going by train to Delhi for an entrance exam. Her resistance to fight came from her stern, athlete-like attitude— whether the fight was with the thieves or with the pain, she was ready.

She said to the doctors that she had already incurred and endured immense pain for over six hours on the tracks and that if they were able to do something in some minutes to help her survive, she was ready to face the pain. Finally, a doctor and a pharmacist gave her a unit of blood each to continue the operation. During the procedure, she was wide awake and felt the pain of getting her leg cut.

Being a national player, she got a lot of media coverage. She was shifted to India's top medical facility known as the 'All India Institute of Medical Sciences,' in New Delhi. She stayed in the trauma center for four months before getting discharged, after which she was free to go.

What's so unique in this story? You may think she was just a normal girl with bad luck who got her leg amputated without anesthesia, and was left physically disabled for all her life. This is the first idea many people will have, but wait till you hear the end of this tragic story.

So, here was Arunima lying in the hospital bed

at AIIMS on her twenty-fifth day in the hospital when she faced another shock. She went through the newspapers and the media coverage, horrified at what she saw. Many news coverages read something like this— "Arunima Sinha: national level athlete jumped off the train because she did not have the ticket when the Train Ticket Examiner asked for it."

This was a complete lie, and she proved it by showing the ticket that she had bought. Then, however, the news coverage changed paths and declared that Arunima tried to commit suicide. She knew that it was a crime, but the media and rumors kept spreading as she tried to prove that she did not commit suicide. When she saw this kind of open rumor-mongering, she shouted and wanted people to hear the truth, but being from a middle-class family, no one listened to her reality, and the mental pain that she suffered made her decide on something.

She believed in herself, and on that day, she decided to take up the most challenging sport of mountaineering and climb to the top of Mount Everest. She took this decision when she lay immobile in the hospital without a leg and several broken limbs.

She became physically disabled, but she had the grit, the commitment, the dedication, and the goal of going to the top of Mount Everest. And you know what? Arunima Sinha did the same within two years! On 11ᵗʰ April 2011, she lost her leg and spent four months in the hospital till August. And on 21ˢᵗ May 2013, she was on top of the world!

How did she do it? It is almost difficult to imagine that a woman with an amputated leg can climb to the top of Mount Everest, on which even the most seasoned mountaineers sometimes surrender and give up. But, Arunima was different. She had her goal crystal clear to her, and she was 'mad' behind it, and that is why she was able to achieve it. She had the determination and the craze of reaching her goal, and she did it. She did it in less than two years of getting discharged from the hospital with a prosthetic leg.

The real, challenging journey for Arunima began when she left the hospital. The dream and vision that she had were so powerful that she did not go back home after discharge; she went to the first Indian woman to climb Mount Everest, Ms. Bachendri Pal. She climbed Everest in 1984, and from then on, she guided people in mountaineering. Arunima went to her in July of 2011, and at first, no one could believe that Arunima could ever climb Mount Everest. Many people told her not to try something like this and get a regular job, but Arunima was stubborn about her decision, and she only had her goal in mind, which is why she went towards it as soon as she was out of the hospital.

When Ms. Bachendri Pal saw Arunima for the first time, she was amazed to see her determination even when Arunima had not fully recovered. She became teary-eyed and said to her, "Arunima, if you can think of taking up a demanding challenge like Everest in this fragile state, then you have already conquered it with your beliefs; now you only need to prove it to the world."

It took a lot of convincing, but she finally got sponsorship for her training in the Nehru Institute of Mountaineering in Uttarkashi. Arunima did not take a single day off from her training from the day she joined. Whether it was a Sunday or a festival, Arunima was always there for her training on time, every day.

It was in this training that she faced the most challenges. In the beginning, it was tough for Arunima as she took three hours for the climb that an average person would do in two minutes. Her prosthetic leg would start bleeding as the wound had not completely healed, and the bones in her right leg had not wholly joined, but she did not stop because of that. When all of this happened, it pained a lot, but she did not, she did not give up, and she continued to train, even if it meant enduring more pain. She felt a little bad when she could not climb at average speed, and here she was, aiming to summit Mount Everest. But she did not stop, and she finally did excel at mountaineering.

However, the tables turned as she trained, and in eight months, she was completing the climbs faster than almost all other people in the institute. The support that she got from Ms. Bachendri Pal empowered her because she was the first to believe in her outside of her family.

But the hurdles were not yet over. Arunima did not have a lot of money, and it was challenging for her to convince people and get full sponsorship for her Everest climb. People rarely believed her, but eventually, she got sponsored by the Tata Steel company, and through them, she was able to prepare for her Everest challenge.

She left for Mount Everest and was the fastest till the rocky area. But when the ice came, her prosthetic leg completely slipped, and it pained, making it difficult for her to hook her shoes in the ice and climb up. She continued to try and get through the ice as little pieces fell out with every feeble kick of hers. After trying many times, a small gap in the ice would develop, and she would use it as a platform to continue her journey to the summit.

She finally reached camp 3 and from there went on to the South Col camp, which was the last one before the summit. Most people give up near or after the South Col camp until the summit, as most deaths happen here. It becomes incredibly challenging to see the people die right in front of you because their oxygen ran out. Arunima had a similar experience as she was climbing through the night. She left the South Col camp and continued upwards. It was dark, and wherever she turned her headlight, she saw dead bodies. At one point on the journey, she saw a Bangladeshi climber's hand moving slightly back and forth as a faint moan came from the mouth. That person was dying, and it broke Arunima's heart to see that the people who had the same goal as hers were dying right next to her. She stood there for 10-15 minutes before taking a pledge. She pledged to summit Mount Everest and said to the dead bodies that she would do it on their behalf and return alive if they could not do it.

She had to step over the bodies and climb because there was no way to go up other than following the rope. She continued to ascend with her guide until he finally stopped her and said, "Arunima, your oxygen is running out; you should return now." At this point, she had reached a place known as Hillary Step, which was only a few climbs below the summit. Arunima felt devastated and was not ready to give up just a few meters away from her goal. She was in a state of ambivalence and knew that if she decided to give up, no one would question or object to her decision because it was a matter of life and death. But she was not ready to give up this golden chance and wanted to achieve her goal, even if her life was at stake. And so, she somehow convinced the guide to continue and go to the top.

After one and a half hours, Arunima, a girl from a middle-class family, a girl without a leg, a girl who was ridiculed by people for her dreams, was the same Arunima who defied all odds and presented it to the world that actually, where there is a will, the way is really there. The same Arunima was at the top of the world at the height of 8848 meters on 21st May 2013 at 10:55 AM!

Arunima says that it was one of the proudest moments for her, and she felt like shouting at the top of her voice to tell everyone that she was finally at the top of the world. Her oxygen was running out, and she asked her guide to take her photo with the Indian flag. Then, she asked him to record a video, but he was agitated because he did not know when her oxygen would run out. He still made the video, and finally, Arunima told him to send the video to India if she did not return alive. Arunima also knew that her oxygen was running out, and she thought that she really might not survive. That is why she wanted the video to reach India and inspire everyone.

They started to descend and they had not gone very far when Arunima's oxygen cylinder ran out, and she fell to the ground, unable to move her body and get up. The guide could not do anything, so he asked her to get up. If she could not, then he would leave her and continue ahead. Most climbers climb Mount Everest at night and don't try to reach the summit after 11 AM because the weather gets bad, and it is often termed as a suicide attempt if one tries to climb that way. The guide could not risk his own life for Arunima. But then, there was a British Climber who saw her as he was going up. He was carrying two oxygen cylinders, and he threw one down for Arunima, which saved her.

The guide quickly helped Arunima and said that she was fortunate to get oxygen near the Everest peak. Then they continued their descend downwards, and at one point, her prosthetic leg completely came off. She tried to move her hands, but they were not moving in the extreme minus temperatures and were red with bleeding. She started to cry and did not know what to do. The guide began to descend downwards on his own, until Arunima put one hand on the rope, and with the other, she gently pushed the prosthetic leg upwards while slowly skimming down. Then, she finally reached a rocky point where she could rest and put the leg back on again.

Most people take 16-17 hours to go from the South Col camp to the summit and back. But, Arunima took 28 hours for the same. Most of the climbers in the South Col camp had thought that Arunima would not return alive. It had been long, and they felt that she too had passed. But all of them were shocked when she came back and finally returned alive.

A physically disabled girl achieved a feat that most of us get afraid of just by thinking of it. This story truly shook me when I read it, and I was amazed by the power of a person's will and determination. Healing from such a severe injury and accident takes years, but Arunima went straight towards her goal and started training after her discharge, and in two years, she did it, and she achieved her goal!

This is the power of meaning and will. This inspiring journey of Arunima Sinha began with the realization of the meaning and purpose of her life. She came to this realization in the hospital when she felt that no one was listening to her, and she wanted to prove that even after the accident, she was capable of doing something. She realized how much emotional pain she had to go through as no one believed in her abilities due to her prosthetic leg. But very few people believed in her because they saw how strong her will was. She wanted to prove that judging a person based on their physical disabilities is wrong because a strong will liberates the disabled body and leverages it to an advantage. But when a person is disabled from the mind and does not accept others' views and abilities, the able body can also not do anything. Empowering those who had lost all hope in life became her purpose, and she did that through her achievements.

She did not stop after conquering Mount Everest

because the goal's achievement was just a single moment. But her purpose, meaning, and will were life-long. Therefore, Arunima continued to climb peaks across the world and decided to scale the highest summits in all continents. She has already climbed these mountains apart from Mount Everest in Asia— Mount Elbrus (Russia), Mount Kilimanjaro (Tanzania), Kosciuszko (Australia), Aconcagua (Argentina), and Mount Vinson (Antarctica). Her strength to persevere through these challenges came from the knowledge of her purpose.

On her website arunimasinha.com, an excerpt from her mission statement reads— "I want to dedicate my achievements "to those who lose hope" so that they never lose heart and achieve their dreams. By conquering all the seven summits I will prove that physical disability can never be a hindrance in achieving your life's goal if you have mental strength, strong will power and firm determination." This statement clearly shows the clarity Arunima has about the meaning in her life. This is the most remarkable example of how powerful a sense of purpose and importance can be in someone's life. Arunima has indeed proved that the meaning in life, combined with the efforts and will power, will surely overcome any physical barrier that may stand in the way.

She has lived by this statement of hers. In her home state of Uttar Pradesh in India, Arunima Sinha has now opened up a school and a sports academy for differently-abled children because she believes that miracles are possible with will-power and determination.

To truly achieve fulfillment and happiness, you need to have the same sense of importance and meaning in your life. When you know that meaning, and you find out whether or not you are working towards it, you will be able to bring in the determination and the will power to succeed, and you will grow when you give in your efforts day and night, just like Arunima.

Finding the meaning and the purpose is, as we know, fundamental and powerful. But many times, people don't know how to find their meaning in life. Like we came to know in the first chapter, you need to look inside yourself to find happiness, meaning, and purpose.

But how to do that? Well, find it out in the next chapter.

3

Why do You Live?

You are walking back home after a tiring day, thinking about which restaurant you would like to order from for dinner, until a stranger comes up to you and abruptly asks— "What is life for?" What will your answer be?

The question will surely stump you, and you even may not be able to find an answer to it quickly. Many people will try to shrug off the interrogator by finding whatever excuse possible and won't think over the question again, considering the inquirer just another student surveying something. Well, that person will be surveying something: how ignorant people are about their reason to live, and this person won't be 'just another student,' but an ignitor of hope to the ones who take the question seriously.

Most of us don't ever answer this question, or even think of it. But, this simple question— "What is life for?" is compellingly powerful; once understood, it can change our lives' trajectory. Why so? Well, because it merely asks us to find the thing that we all are looking for: meaning. Consider this question to be the last one you need to answer to pass the most crucial exam of your life and treat it with the seriousness it deserves. Think about this question right now, and try to find the answer.

If you can't find the answer right now, don't worry. Let that question sit in your mind, seep in, and the answer will come to you. It may be even in the most unexpected circumstances— no wonder the most incredible ideas come in the bathtub (Eureka!) and under the apple tree ☺, making you jump up and down with the joy of finding the answer!

Now, all you need to do is think about this question and try to answer it; no matter how vague, raw, or childish your answer may seem, you don't need to judge it. It is important to remember that there is no one to evaluate your answer and classify it as right or wrong. Everyone's answer is different, and everyone's meaning of life is different. It is essential to know what life is for, but it isn't imperative to classify and judge it. All you need to do is find your answer and live by it.

If Arunima had allowed other people's judgments about her goal and her meaning to affect her, she would not have been able to climb the Everest and multiple other peaks today. In the same way, you also don't need to let other people's judgments affect you.

Leading a meaningful life is essential, and this question is the first step towards it, and it is often taking the first step that makes all the difference!

Answering this question for yourself and finding the meaning of life is an excellent achievement in itself. However, if knowing the meaning and purpose of living is often one of the most essential things we need to be clear about, why is it a great achievement?

Well, in today's world, we are growing socially closer and internally distant. What does this mean? In the social media age, everything connects over the internet, and it is becoming challenging for us to communicate with ourselves, while it is much easier to communicate with others. We are just one click away from knowing what is happening in other people's lives, but we often don't realize that we are only one click away from connecting with ourselves as well by turning off the phone, laptop, and iPad for some time. When we have the choice to connect with ourselves, why don't we do that?

We have conditioned our minds to make us feel left out when we don't have the latest information, which is why we choose to click on the apps and see what's happening instead of clicking on the power button and connecting with ourselves. To find out the meaning of the life you have been living for such a long time, you need to disconnect from this constantly hyped-up world and find bliss in being left out.

In the first chapter, we discussed that we need to look into ourselves to find happiness and meaning instead of looking outwards. Now, you may be wondering that to look inside yourself, you need to do a lot of things. Well, ironically, all you need to do is not do anything and let your mind wander for some time. Yes, it is all you need to do to connect with yourself. To find the answer to the question that random yet thoughtful interrogator asked you, you need to drop everything and observe the wildness of your mind.

Every day, we have thousands and thousands of thoughts running through our minds, and we can't process them all. That is why many thoughts just come and pass by, and the important ones crowd upon our mental priority lists. What happens to those many thoughts that go inside our minds? Well, they get stored, and when that happens, it takes up mental space, just like anything else does. Positive or negative, important or unimportant, almost all of our thoughts are stored inside us, and the storage is limited. How many books can you shove into a cabin? Limited, right? It is the same with the mind.

When these thoughts accumulate and accumulate, the mind runs wildly through them and does not understand which ones are important and which ones aren't. This often happens when there is a lot of mental pressure and energy usage. These high-tension moments make our thoughts run wild, beginning an endless loop of thinking in our minds. Our mind is like a jungle full of monkey-like thoughts. Whenever there is a lot of confusion and distress in this jungle, the monkeys run wild, and therefore it is called the wild monkey mind!

Imagine gathering a spillage of marble balls across a living room. You need to look everywhere, under the carpet, under the table, under the sofa and even in other rooms and under their furniture if their doors were open. This becomes hectic, right?

It is the same when we try to control our thoughts and cage them like monkeys. They will shriek and shout and scream and bang, do whatever is possible to go free, and they will eventually make us give up and allow them to go away when we continue with our work. This happens when we try to control our thoughts and calm down by "not thinking" about those thoughts.

Do this small activity along with me. I want you to read this and close your eyes for a minute. You don't have to think about a pink elephant with an orange tail, walking over blue water with a green alien dancing on its top. Don't think of this for the next one minute and close your eyes.

What did you think? You most probably thought of the elephant all the time while trying to tell yourself to shut up and not think about the elephant!

This is what happens when we choose to not think about some thought. And this is why trying to control thoughts is not the way; welcoming them is. How so? Well, when you hate or detest a thought, it does not like it, so it simply reciprocates and troubles you even more.

But when you welcome a thought and accept it as a part of you without judgment, then the thought will become a friend of yours and will silence down its retaliation and protest. To get over the shrieking monkeys in the jungle of your mind, you need to give them an affectionate hug and let them free. They will go away to their own lives without disturbing yours. And soon, your mind will silence down into clarity as you free each monkey.

Take a break, sit down, close your eyes, and do

nothing. Remember, don't do anything and just let the thoughts in your mind come and go. The thoughts will ramble and bubble a lot, but you just let them. This is a way of clearing out the clutter. Once you start practicing this habit of consciously being left out for some time, you will understand yourself because the wild monkeys will leave and sparse out. When the monkeys are gone, there will be silence and a chance for you to connect with yourself. When you connect with yourself and understand who you are, you will find out what life is for.

When you declutter your mind, you will be able to find what you live for, and you will be able to answer that stranger who came up to you at the beginning of this chapter! In the coming chapter, we will discuss how to find the purpose and passion in life to understand what you want to do.

4

Passion and Purpose

"When you feel an impulse to do something that is so strong, so undeniable that you can't do anything else without thinking of it, it has a very high probability of being your calling, your purpose. Don't ignore it. Think about it. That action can lead you to happiness and peace."

—Piyush Kolhe

Meaning, passion, and purpose are all very interlinked notions. Our understanding of ourselves and the change that we wish to create in the world determine our meaning and purpose. While our passion is a skill-set that we develop or possess to fulfill that meaning and purpose, for me, my meaning and purpose in life is understanding and spreading positivity to as many people as possible. My passion is writing, and I am creating a profession by combining my passion and my purpose. In this chapter, we will be learning how to do that.

But before that, do you want to take on another exciting story? This time, we will understand the 'why' behind meaning by seeing how it emerged in our lives and how we have been fulfilling it. This understanding will also help us in understanding our passion and purpose.

Here is Adam. Living about 30,000 years ago in the Mediterranean forest plains, foraging for food day in and day out. Living a meaningful life has been the essence of existence itself. For animals, living a meaningful life means not getting killed by a predator and making sure that the species continues and flourishes. Apart from survival and reproduction, there isn't much that animals do to live a meaningful life. And in Adam's time, people are no different than the animals. Adam searches for food, escapes predators, and makes sure that his species thrives. Apart from that, he has virtually no impact on himself or his life. He lives this way until one day, he forgets the path back to his tribe, and a pride of hungry lions take advantage of that and kill him.

He suffers that pain and feeling of being torn apart alive as his soul levitates out of his body. He sees a beam of light and heads towards it, which takes him to the heaven where God sits. God speaks something in a language Adam has never heard before but still wholly understands. He tries to reply and does it in the same language with fluency. He doesn't know what is happening but is happy that communication and understanding exist.

God says to him, "Dear Adam, you have been a great warrior in your lifetime, and I am sorry for your untimely demise. Here, as a token of apology, I give you the chance to prepare yourself mentally by having a pre-glimpse of the new world. This is Mark from France, who died in a fatal car crash in Pennsylvania. He will explain to you how the modern world works.

Adam is confused but replies in a faint, ambivalent tone, "Okay."

"Mark! Come out here!" God shouts as he completely ignores Adam's acknowledgment. But Adam doesn't care because he is more excited to know about the new world.

"Hey! I am Mark." The voice from behind him says, "I am here to explain to you the importance of meaning in the world that is 30,000 years ahead of yours. Things have changed a lot lately, but one thing has changed the most— the sense of meaning. Animals and you people only ate food and continued to take the species forward without any definite purpose to life; you just lived.

"However, we humans are different. Survival and reproduction are still the basic things that make us meaningful as organisms. But, our cognitive powers allow us to follow and pursue a greater purpose and meaning in life. Let me show you how our mental progress has made us capable of following more profound and complex endeavors than animals. In today's world, basic survival is easily possible because we don't live out in the open jungle anymore, but in well organized and sophisticated societies— which you don't know of. Now, if our cognitive senses had not evolved, we would not have been able to form such complex communities. However, if the rapid development had happened without our mental progress, we would have led unmeaningful and random lives without direction because we would not have to worry about survival anymore. Our minds would not have had anything to work for, and that would have made us only useless creatures, whom nature would have preferred wiping out. Fortunately, this isn't the real story because if it were, we would not exist..."

As Mark continues, Adam understands bits because Mark's explanation is entirely unknown and new. "So, humans eventually found a way to use their cognitive abilities, where they lived meaningfully by doing something beneficial to anybody or anything on this planet. Columbus is a great example— the person you again would not know, but just get the idea! Now, what reason did he have to take a courageous voyage across the world? It was simply to find a sea route to the east to help the Europeans get spices and other essential materials easily. This is just one of an infinite number of examples that date back to multiple millennia. But what do you need to learn from this? You may be wondering. Well, you need to learn that the cognitive powers you get need to be used in the right manner to sculpt the meaning and purpose of your existence."

Adam is still confused. God says, "Mark, you did a terrible job at explaining, but Adam, I hope you got the gist of it." Adam nods and then is quickly pulled upwards into a chamber where a team of doctors tries to wipe his memories off. Bye!

What Mark said will be difficult to understand for Adam, but not for us, because we live in Mark's age. We now know that our cognitive powers have enabled us to do great things, but very few of us use it in the right way to create something meaningful.

Look around you. How many people around you are building or doing something meaningful? It doesn't necessarily mean that it is something philanthropic or something that contributes to the world at a large scale— it can only positively impact that specific person. That is also something meaningful. I assume that the number of people doing something meaningful in their lives around you is very few.

The reason behind this? Many are not aware of this fact at all. Life is a precious gift and squandering it by doing valueless and unlikeable things is the worst possible use of it. Now, you are aware of this fact, and by understanding it correctly, you will know what you want to do.

The best way to use your cognitive powers is to do something meaningful that adds value. A big question here is— how can that be done? Well, it is simple. You need to know what you want to do— that is, finding your meaning and purpose. The two ways you can find your purpose are— one, by understanding yourself, which we already learned, and second, by being curious.

To take my example, I am a fourteen-year-old student, and I got into writing last year. In 2018, when I was in the sixth class, I thought of becoming a motivational speaker because I was always intrigued by the different motivational speakers that I saw over the internet. I felt as if that was my calling and that I wanted to inspire people to take action and improve themselves. In a way, I was trying to spread positivity. I was excelling in school and became a part of the student council for the second consecutive year, and through that, I also learned that I had leadership qualities. In the class, I socialized a lot and was always ready to help everyone around me, which helped me realize that I was an outgoing person. I carried the thought of becoming a motivational speaker to fulfill my calling, and it slowly slipped away because I shifted to other things like keeping up with the school work.

Then, in July of 2019 (almost a year after I decided to become a motivational speaker), I discussed twenty-first-century digital skills with my mom and explored them on the internet. Finally, I came across the skill of blogging and felt particularly interested in it. On that same evening, I researched a little more about it, went over to wordpress.com, registered for a free domain, and wrote my first blog on habits.

Now, this small conversation and a little curiosity completely changed the trajectory of my life. The thought of inspiring people by becoming a motivational speaker had subsided, but I had buried this seed in my mind, and it came out in this way! I got incredibly excited about writing, and this small incident completely changed the way I thought about inspiring people. Through my blog website, I understood that I had the power to inspire people worldwide by writing blog posts. With each post, I became clearer and more precise in my expression and wrote various posts on different aspects of life in which people faced problems. I became deeply interested in writing, and today, that discussion, that curiosity, and that seed of doing something meaningful turned me into an author and made this book possible!

What did I do to find out what my passion was?

I simply looked into myself and searched for what it is that interested me. To do this, simply look into yourself and write down the things you enjoy doing because your purpose and meaning lie in what you like to do and feel energetic while doing. It can be anything from dance to writing, from researching to cycling, and from swimming to teaching others. Whatever it is that you enjoy doing, recognize it.

Also, you may not be doing the thing that interests you, but you may be watching other people do it, and you admire them.

This happened to me too, as I wasn't doing motivational speaking, but I watched other people do it, which inspired me. You may be inspired by LeBron James even though you don't play basketball as of now, and you dream of playing it at that level one day. Now, that is something in which you may develop a genuine interest! This way, talk to yourself and discover your passion.

Before I started blogging, I could never have imagined that I will get into such a thing where I expressed my thoughts by simply writing them out on the internet. I never consciously thought of blogging before, but I still found out that I wanted to do this. How did I find that out? Well, it happened because I was curious. I explored multiple things until I stumbled upon blogging and decided to do it.

Curiosity is vital to discover your purpose. We learned that passion is the skill-set that we have or develop to make our purpose our reality. But often, it is the discovery of the passion that leads to the discovery of the purpose. I was curious, and I experimented with blogging; I liked it and enjoyed doing it, and after discovering the passion, I was able to find the underlying meaning and purpose that shaped my life. If you don't find what you want to do even after reflecting on what you like, you will benefit from being curious.

How can you be curious? Find out about different things. For example, if you stumble upon a person's profile on Twitter who is teaching something on digital coaching and consulting, try that out if it generates a sense of engagement in you. If you find it interesting, continue, and you may find precisely what you want to do, and if not, then drop it. You can also decide to study or experience a specific thing for three months. After acquiring the skills associated with it, you can determine whether you want to continue using the skill or not.

Curiosity has been a part of us since primitive times. If we were not curious, we would not have discovered fire. If we were not curious, we wouldn't have known why everything sticks to the ground, and if we were not curious, we wouldn't have been able to enjoy dinner with our family without worrying about the oil lamp going off.

It is only because our ancestors were curious that we can eat delicious and cooked food today. It is only because of Newton's inquisitive nature that we know how gravity works, and we have been able to use that to erect complex structures all across the globe. It is only because of Thomas Edison's curious experiment with the electric battery that we can see everything around us at night when it is dark. Being curious is one of the best ways to find meaningful things that are there for you to learn and practice.

Be curious and search for what you like, and then you will have the first key to creating something meaningful out of life!

If you have a passion but not a skill out of it yet (just like my passion for blogging), you need to learn how to make that passion a skill, and by doing that, you will be able to bring your purpose into reality!

When I found out that inspiring others by writing was my passion, I started practicing it to form a skill. After I set up my website on wordpress.com, I decided to write two blogs a month and each time on a different topic. I wrote two blogs in July, then in August, September, and October as well. After that, I wrote one blog in November and did not write any in December and January. In February, I wrote again, and finally, in March, I decided to write one blog every week, and I have been writing a blog a week from then on without fail. Even though my journey wasn't smooth, I have learned a lot from writing forty-six blog posts till now. My prose and clarity in expression improved with every blog post, which gave me the courage to write this book and share it with you.

Finding your passion and understanding what clicks with you is immensely important, but turning it into a skill is also very important. Turning your passion into a skill means having excellent command of your specific field of interest. If playing basketball is your passion and you dream of being a star player one day but haven't started playing it professionally yet, it is just a passion that you need to develop. There will be numerous people who will have the same dream, but few like LeBron James will deliberately practice and put in hours of hard work to make this passion a skill by gaining confidence and mastery in basketball. So, you need to put in deliberate hours of hard work into your passion and hone it into a skill because that is when you truly gain expertise and excellence in that specific field.

I am still practicing my writing skill, and it will improve with every blog and every book that I publish. As I walk this path and try to improve and gain excellence in my specific passion, I invite you to walk this path with me and transform your passion into a skill. Why not do it together? I promise you that it will be a journey of a lifetime, and the hours that you put into making your passion a skill will compound over and over to give you great returns.

We improve maths only with practice, which is precisely the case with everything else in our lives. That is why corporates prefer to hire experienced employees instead of the ones who are just starting. Because skilled employees have the practice and excellence in that specific field, they will thus be more beneficial to the company. Your deliberate practice to turn your passion into a skill will reward you in the same way. The more training and experience you will have, the more sophisticated and excellent you will be with that skill.

A critical question that comes up when practicing and honing your passion is: to what extent do you need to sharpen your passion-related skill? The answer is— as much as possible. There are two things we expect to achieve as a result of doing something: perfection and excellence. However, instead of getting these two things, we often get disappointment and discontentment with our work. And this can happen when trying to hone a skill as well. The results don't turn out to be as expected. You may wonder, why does this feeling of disappointment arise instead of what we had hoped for (that is, the highest level of perfection in the skill we are trying to hone)? Well, this happens because we chose the wrong thing to expect in the first place. The reason for our disappointment is chasing perfection; let's understand why.

To truly understand why chasing perfection leads to disappointment, we need to understand the real meaning of the word 'perfect.' Many people use this word to define something that is truly unbeatable and is at the zenith of beauty and glory. We cannot improve anything perfect anymore because it is at the pinnacle of how deep and glorified it can be. Perfection is being at such a high level that there is no way for you to improve and raise the bar of perfection any higher. It is the ultimate level one can reach, and there is nothing beyond it. This is perfection in its true essence.

However, there is one problem with the concept of perfection itself. In the real world, the bar that defines perfection doesn't exist, and there is always scope for improving and excelling because the world is continuously evolving. This is why the concept of perfection doesn't match with how our world works. If everything was perfect, what was the need for volcanic eruptions to wipe out the old landforms and form entirely new ones? If everything was perfect, then why did the earth transition from the ice age to the way it is today? If everything was perfect, then what was the need for early humans to settle down and cultivate food instead of continuing to forage for it? If everything was perfect, then what was the need of inventing technology and automation?

This is the problem. We expect to achieve something that doesn't exist. It is like being a kid who goes to a horse-riding academy and demands to ride on a unicorn. We all know that the unicorn doesn't exist and think that the child is silly. However, we try to find perfection in a world where it doesn't exist, just like the kid trying to find a unicorn amidst the horse stables. Therefore, don't all of us deserve to be called silly and childish?

Yes, we do. But how many of us really want to be called silly and childish? None of us, right? That is why we need to realize that we can neither chase perfection nor achieve it. When we try to pursue perfection, we always end up disappointing ourselves.

So, if perfection doesn't exist, what makes people successful and fulfill their purpose? The answer is excellence. There is a fragile line between excellence and perfection. And in the chase for perfection, we tend to smudge the line, and then it becomes difficult to figure out its exact location. It is essential to keep this thin line clear and distinct because excellence will give us success and mastery.

What is excellence, you may ask? Excellence simply means highly qualitative or extremely good. It is one of the highest levels of fineness and understanding of something, but it is not perfect. Even when someone excels at something, there are always areas where that person has the chance to notch up a little and improve a bit more.

Constant improvement will create excellence and mastery because things change very quickly in our ever-evolving world. That's why perfection doesn't exist. Evolution and change require flow, but perfection brings stagnation. This significant difference makes them incompatible, and therefore, perfection and evolution can't exist together.

However, you can still achieve mastery in something by striving for excellence, expecting to reach a level where you create excellent quality and intricate depth. To strive for excellence is ideal because you show the zeal to improve the things you excel in constantly. Richard Feynman was a great physicist who had devised a particularly great technique to learn anything. It was known as the Feynman Learning Technique. He said that to learn anything, you need to pretend as if you are explaining it to a young child. To do that, you will need to describe it as simply as you can, and if you are not able to, you need to revisit the concept and learn it again. It's a great technique applicable to learning a skill as well. When you practice a skill, you will know you have gained expertise when you teach it to a young child with immense simplicity, starting from the very basics to the more complicated things. By practicing your ability to explain your particular skill to a small child, you can find out the areas where you need to notch up and understand your skill a little better. Richard

Feynman himself was a great example of this. He explained mathematics from the basics all the way to the fundamentals of pre-calculus in four pages! He went this deep into simplifying things!

One of the most outstanding examples of striving for excellence in the corporate world is Apple. When the company introduced the first iPhone in 2007, everyone thought that Apple had completely revolutionized the world of technology. To people at that time, this was the highest level at which pocket technology could go. But Apple did not stop there because it knew that the iPhone wasn't perfect. Apple still knew that even though it had achieved excellence with the iPhone's formation, there was scope for improvement. Just because Apple took this approach towards their creation and improved it year after year, it became possible for the company to stay at the top. And now we all know how different the latest iPhone is from the first one!

If Apple thought in 2007 that its iPhone was perfect and that there was no need to bring improvements, would it have succeeded at being excellent for all this time? The answer is no because other companies would have seized the opportunity and created better products while Apple would have kept thinking that its iPhone was the best. Finally, they would have realized that the other companies have made better products than the iPhone and that its popularity has decreased. This is why it is essential to improve and become excellent, not perfect.

As an author, I am not perfect in writing, but with every writing session that I put in, I can excel and improve this skill more and more. Continuously improve your skills, and you will surely find yourself gaining expertise and excellence soon!

Part Two

Gearing Up! Preparing to Take Action Towards the Passion!

5

Goals and Preparation: Why are They Important?

How do you make pasta? Very simple, right? You chop the garlic, the tomatoes, and other vegetables. You pull out the pasta from the packet and boil it. Then, you chop things to make the sauce, and finally, you mix it all to create delicious pasta topped up with cheese and fresh parsley.

Now, I have a little challenge for you, and you can take it up if you want to (entirely voluntary). So, I want you to make pasta, but with a little twist. You won't be allowed to see any recipe or follow any exact way of cooking, and you will not have any time to prepare the ingredients by chopping them, boiling them, blanching them, etc. All you can do is put the pan on the stove and start cooking the pasta right away.

Most of you will say that it is just not possible to do something like that. And I agree with you. I know that it is not possible to cook pasta this way or to cook anything this way. Prior preparation is always needed to cook something delicious and to cook something edible. We cannot just toss in the pasta, the garlic, the tomatoes, the onions, the spices, and the other ingredients directly into the pan to make pasta. We need to change them in some way or the other, combine them in a particular way and then cook in a specific way to make sure that we have indeed cooked pasta!

If we can set a clear goal, follow the right methods, and prepare beforehand for cooking, why not in life? Many people expect to get results as soon as they take the first step towards something, and that is why we are always in a hurry to take that first step. To get results faster, we tend to ignore the importance of preparation and goal-setting.

If we compare pasta making to life, we can say that we want to eat delicious pasta as soon as we pull out the pasta packet. Does it seem rational and realistic? No, right? But we expect something like this in life. It does not make sense for us to eat the pasta as soon as we take the first step by pulling out the packet. We need to wait, we need to prepare, and we need to persist in reaping the best results and eating the tastiest pasta.

Preparing and planning your actions from your passion's foundation is very important because you cannot know how to go towards your goal without knowing where you stand. If you are an engineer who is building a two-story living compound, will you start from the roof or the foundation below? The obvious answer is the foundation. If you were to start building the top first, you would never be able to finish the building because as soon as you would finish making the roof, it would collapse as there is nothing to support it. Very logical, right?

Now, imagine that you have to start building the foundation, and there is a natural pit in the place, so you will begin by modifying that pit a little, and you will fill in the foundation. But what if you don't have this and you have some leveled bare soil? Then you will start by digging a pit in the ground and pouring in the foundation. But, if you have a tree-covered area on which you need to make the foundation, you can't just start by pouring the foundation. You need to get the trees cut, then you need to get a pit made in that place, and finally, you can then pour in the foundation. Therefore, planning and preparing are essential. Even if you have to do the same thing someone else is doing, you must know where you currently stand; otherwise, you will just be pouring cemented foundation over tall trees and then hoping to build a house on that.

If you want to learn how to cook pasta, but you

have never cooked before, then you need to know the basics first— how to handle the pans and the heat while maintaining safety with the flame and, above all, learning how to chop the ingredients without cutting your finger. You need to know all of these things first before cooking pasta because these are the foundations of cooking. It will be il-logical to go and start cooking pasta on your first visit to the kitchen.

Once you know where you stand, you need to see how you can get to your destination. But do you know where it is that you want to go? When you try to cook pasta by directly heating the pan and not following any cooking and preparation method, you will have nothing but a very vague idea of what you want to cook. It is the same with life when you try to take action without planning, preparation, or path clarity. You want to get re-sults in your life, but without knowing where you stand right now and preparing for the journey, how can you expect to get the results you want? For this you need to have goals in life. A goal gives meaning and direction to actions, and without one, you cannot achieve the results you want, no matter how much hard work you put in. Even the most hard-working person will be nothing more than a mule carrying people up and down the hill without clear direction.

Football is one of the greatest examples in which the importance of having a clear direction is visi-ble. One of the greatest and the most famous players in modern football history is Cristiano Ronaldo. Almost every person knows this renowned footballer. He has scored over 600 goals in his career, which is a lot! Now, just imagine that there is one fine match in which Ronaldo has scored six goals all by himself, but he doesn't know which goal will benefit his team and which one won't. He feels great about having scored six goals, but at the end of the match, he realizes that he had been scoring for the opponent team all along, and he did not know that.

Will people consider Ronaldo to be a great player if this happened throughout his career? Would he have been able to do so much and achieve so much? The answer is no, and that's why the right direction is vital in life. All your efforts will go in vain if you don't have a clear and specific direction in your life. You decide whether you want to be a little patient and plan out your actions according to your path or if you want to let your efforts go down in vain.

Having a clear and specific direction is the first step in preparing for your goal. After that, you need to plan out your actions with rationality, belief, and confidence.

Now that you know how important it is to plan and prepare patiently with a clear goal in mind, we will be exploring how to do that in the coming chapters. The number one skill that you need to learn is how to set a goal the right way. It is just like chopping onion and garlic for making pasta. If you do it right, the reward for you will be delicious pasta, and if you do it wrong, the reward will be a band-aid over your finger.

6

How to Set Goals the Right Way

Would you believe me if I told you that a person in this world could predict how your future will be? Would you believe me? Maybe you would; perhaps you wouldn't. But you will not be entirely sure of the amount of truth in this statement, right? Yes, because we have certain connotations with fortune-telling. Some think it is just a stereotype, while others have a steadfast belief in it. We believe many different things and don't believe some, especially about the unpredictable and unknown future. But trust my words, there is a person on this planet who has a very fair idea of how your future will be.

I know you are thinking that I am playing some

trick on you, but no.

There is a person.

That person is you.

Yes, you are the only person on this planet who has a fair idea of what your life will turn out to be. Don't understand? Read on.

How do you know about your future? Because your goals and your present actions define your future. You can do a simple self-analysis and understand how your current actions will determine your future. If you have a goal and are working towards it, you are probably on the path to achieving it. If you don't have a goal, you are not on the way towards fulfilling the meaning and purpose in your life. You need to set the right goals because they will give you the direction you need in life.

Goal setting is essential, but doing it the right way is what shapes all the difference. Even if you have set the right goal for yourself, but you have done it wrongly, you won't reap good results. One of the most important things that you need to do is being specific while setting goals. Imagine that you are traveling to California, and you don't know about the places or the landmarks in Los Angeles, and your GPS has stopped working. You remember that your hotel is on Olympic Boulevard. Now, you ask some people for directions, and they give you replies like,

- Oh! That street is just a few miles down the second road from here.

- That street? It is just around a few corners from here.

- How did you end up here? That place is across the city. You should go right down this main city road.

- That place is just nearby. You need to turn to the left, go down the road for around fifteen to twenty miles, and the road on the right is Olympic Boulevard.

Do you think you will ever be able to reach the place you are looking for with these kinds of directions? No, as you don't know what to do. You will spend your whole day trying to find your place instead of simply relaxing and enjoying your vacation until you come up to a stranger who is kind enough to give you the details.

The stranger says, "Okay! So, you want to go to Olympic Boulevard, right? First of all, you need to know that you are in Lakewood right now, and Olympic Boulevard is around 22 miles from here. First, you need to get onto Clark Avenue and from there turn right onto the Artesia freeway. Then take the next exit to Interstate-605 and continue onto the Santa Ana Freeway. Finally, turn to the Santa Monica freeway at the major junction, and after a few miles, turn right onto the LA Live way. It will lead you straight to West Olympic Boulevard, and you can get on it by turning right."

These are some precise directions, which we need to know while setting goals. We need to be very specific. When there is a lack of clarity and ambiguity, the mind gets confused and doesn't know where to go. This confusion then doesn't allow the mind to get the exact information, and because of that, even after knowing where you want to go, you end up in the wrong place.

So, now let us understand how to set a goal. We all must have learned about five 'W's and one 'H' in school, and this concept is helpful in life, especially in setting goals. To select a goal properly, we need to answer these five 'W's and one 'H.' We will be forming a written goal statement at the end of this explanation as we understand what we genuinely want to achieve.

1. ***What.*** The first thing you need to understand is the "what" in your goal statement. You need to know what it is that you want to do before doing anything! Let's look at a couple of examples. For this book, the "what" part of my goal statement would be writing and finishing my book. This point is as simple as that. If you want to become a great basketball player, you need to practice, and

your goal statement's "what" part can be playing basketball.

2. **_Why._** Now, you need to know why you have decided to do something as the meaning is important. If the purpose of the action does not align with your passion, you will not feel fulfilled and happy in doing it. For me, when I combine the "what' with the "why," my goal statement goes something like this— "I want to write and finish this book because I want to help people improve their lives by finding meaning, happiness, and fulfillment." My goal statement would look like this. Let us take another example. If you want to excel at your job, you need to be specific. Just saying, "I want to excel at my job" won't work. You must know what you want to do to excel and why you want to do it. For example, you may say, "I want to increase my efficiency at work and double my work speed so that I can earn more at the same time and provide abundantly to my family." This statement is very apt and specific in terms of the "what" and the "why."

3. **_When._** The "when" aspect of goal setting is hugely relevant because you will not achieve your goal without a defined time frame. Let's say that I have decided to write a book and that is what I want to do. I know why I want to do it, and I start doing it. Do you think I

will be able to finish it? Yes, I will be, but I may procrastinate and delay the whole project for a long time. Therefore, the "when" part of the goal setting is crucial. When you have a timeline on your goal, you instruct your mind to take quick action with preparation. With the concept of a timeline to finish and achieve your goal, you somewhat inculcate a sense of gamification to your goal. Gamification includes a sense of competitiveness in the process of achieving your goal. So, when you gamify the experience, you race against time, bringing in the sense of thrill and enjoyment by finishing the task before the deadline. You will also not feel bored while doing something because the deadline will keep you going. This way, you will not be uncertain about finishing that specific thing, and you will also be able to train your mind to get work done in a limited amount of time. For example, I will form my goal statement for writing this book like, "I want to write and finish this book by 1st December 2020 to help people improve their lives by finding meaning, happiness, and fulfillment."

4. **Who.** Using the pronoun "I," you affirm that you will take action, which mostly answers this part of the goal-setting process. But there will be times when your goal and its process will impact other people. If it is a

significant impact, then you can mention it in your goal statement. Remember the second example from the "why" section? It was this— "I want to increase my efficiency at work and double my work speed so that I can earn more at the same time and provide abundantly to my family." In this goal statement, the consequence or the why is affecting the person's family very directly, and therefore it is mentioned here. In my goal statement as well, the result of me writing this book will directly affect the reader who reads it, which is you in this case. I have mentioned it in my goal statement as well by saying, "I want to write and finish this book by 1st December 2020 to help people improve their lives by finding meaning, happiness, and fulfillment." In this statement, I have mentioned how the people who read this book will be affected. If there is something like this with your goal, you can mention it to know where you are heading, specifically.

5. **How.** Now, it is time for us to understand another vital aspect of goal-setting— the "how" aspect. After possessing the appropriate knowledge, if you don't know how to work towards your goal, how will you achieve it? When you mention how you will achieve your goal in your statement, you

form a guideline and a track for yourself that you can frequently use to understand if you are taking the right actions. In my goal statement, I will mention the "how" this way— "I want to write and finish a book by 1st December 2020 to help people improve their lives by finding meaning, happiness, and fulfillment. I will do it by opening my laptop every day and typing in a Microsoft Word Document." . The "how" aspect will help you know if your actions align with your goal or not. Let's say I had this goal in mind, but I did not write about how I would proceed. Then maybe I would have been confused with which word processing software to use as well. I know it sounds silly, but it is true; being specific saves a lot of time and energy, allowing you to get right into the task of working towards your goal.

6. **Where.** Yes! You have finally come to the last step of setting up your goal statement, the "where" aspect. It would be best if you mentioned where you would take action towards your goal. It will not happen in that exact place all the time, but knowing an ideal location is essential. For example, if your goal is to play basketball, you cannot train in your bedroom, right? You need to go to the academy or the sports center to practice and train. Suppose your goal statement is, "I want to become a good basketball player in 2

years by practicing every day." We can add the location or the "where" aspect to this by forming a goal statement like, "I want to become a good basketball player in two years by practicing every day at the local sports club." This statement completes the circle of forming very specific and to-the-point goals that help you step right into the action with preparation.

Now, my complete goal statement for writing this book would be, "I want to write and finish a book by 1st December 2020 to help people improve their lives by finding meaning, happiness, and fulfillment. I will do it by opening my laptop every day and typing in a Microsoft Word Document sitting on my desk in the study room." You need to formulate straight, simple, and specific statements to achieve your goals and fulfill your meaning.

Now you know how to set goals the right way. Remember, you need to be clear, direct, specific, and need to answer the six questions related to making goal statements. Live by these statements and fulfill the timelines you have set. Don't let ambiguity and confusion set in because you will lose your precious time making amendments to your goal, leading to more mental confusion and less work. Spend some time to understand how to set goals and set them precisely so that there is nothing capable of stopping you when you launch into action!

7

The Path to Proper Planning

You now know your passion, and you know how to form the right goals to help you go towards it. Being specific and knowing what you want to do in a goal statement is like having a rough plan to proceed towards your goal. But you need to have a proper plan, and you need to know how to form it in the right manner. In this chapter, we are going to look at just that.

If I were to ask you what a plan is, what would be your answer? One of the most probable answers is: a plan is a pathway that one follows to do something. For cooking pasta, there is a plan. To go from 'place A' to 'place B,' there is a plan. There is a plan for losing weight, and for writing a book, there is a plan. All you need to do is learn how to devise the one that suits you the most.

Making a plan is not difficult; it is a straightforward process, but only when you have complete clarity and understanding of what you want to do or make. Let's say you want to make a burger, but you don't know if you're going to make a leafy one or a cheesy one. Then it will become difficult for you to plan out the whole recipe and decide whether you want to have more cheese or more lettuce, and in the end, you may not have a great burger. But, if you knew that you had to create a cheese-loaded burger for a party, you would buy top-quality cheese from the market, and that will help you make sure that you make the best cheeseburger in your capacity.

Imagine that you are filing a resume for a job that you love to do. You set out a goal to get the job by improving your communication skills and creating a great resume. To do this the right way and grab your prospective employers' attention, you should make the resume reflect the quality that a specific employer is seeking in you. Therefore, when you decide how to make your resume, you must keep your prospective employer in mind. If one employer is looking for excellence in work, your resume should reflect that. However, if another employer is looking for maximum productivity, then your resume should reflect that. It is just like deciding whether to put more lettuce or more cheese in your burger.

So, how do you plan the right way? There are various steps that you need to reflect upon, and these will help you form an outline for your over-all and daily actions. Are you ready to take charge of how your days turn out to be? If yes, then here you go: -

1. ***Understand. Understand. Understand.*** One of the first things you need to do is understand what you are trying to build or do from its very basic. You need to understand what kind of effort it demands, what kind of energy and time that specific goal needs, and if you can give it that much or not. You need to question things and try to find the answers to deeply understand "why" some things will work and why some others won't. It is crucial to clearly understand whether the burger you are trying to make is a cheeseburger or a healthy burger. You need to know whether you are making a resume for an employer who demands results or an employer who requires formality and punctuality.

I need to know whether my book is for intellectual or mental stimulation or for people trying to find solutions. I need to know all of this and understand the different aspects of my book writing, like how much time it will take to edit and write my book, how long it will be, and when I will publish it. This kind of understanding is essential, no matter what it is that you do.

2. ***Know where you stand.*** In the fifth chapter, we discussed that knowing your current position is important to begin your journey towards your goal, and that is why you must understand how to find out where you currently stand.

For example, when I had to plan how to achieve my writing goal and publish this book, I needed to know where my position was back then. I knew that I had a good understanding of my genre, but I had never written something with immense depth. To develop my knowledge, I compared my current position to various successful authors like Anthony Robbins, Jay Shetty, and Robin Sharma. When Jay Shetty published his book, he already had a large social media presence and following. When Anthony Robbins published his books, he had a large public following that he built through his coaching program, while Robin Sharma started out differently.

On the other hand, I did not have any of these things, and therefore, I realized that I need to start my career from scratch and do it differently from other successful authors. If I were to blindly follow Jay Shetty's strategy of sharing the book to his audience for pre-ordering, I would not have achieved the success he did because I did not have a large fanbase as he did. From this, I understood that even if the goal were the same, the process of achieving it would be different for every person. You can realize this by researching some people who are doing the same thing you are— find out how they began and compare it with where you are. If you already have good prior knowledge of the field you are entering, you can take that as your base and start working towards your goal. You need to find out where you stand.

3. ***If you feel confused, let it out.*** Often in this process, there may be times when you feel lost, confused, stuck, or unable to make a decision. It will help if you do not let the whirlpool of confusion play like an audiotape in your mind in these situations. You need to let it out— not on some person— but some paper, because if you feel others may judge you because of your confusion and worries, then the paper won't do that; it is not a person. Just write about all of your dilemmas and don't interrupt your thoughts. Let the volcano of confusions erupt and after all the lava has flown out in the form of words, look at the paper again, read through the chaos you have written down. You will be able to develop clarity, leading you towards the solution. Then simply tear off the paper and throw it in the dustbin. This way, you are throwing confusion and negativity into the

dustbin— away from your life. So, whenever you feel stuck and confused, let that confusion come out on paper, and as you write, you will come to know that the answers are at hand, and you will always find yours.

4. ***Write down the things you need to do.*** After learning all these things, you now have to outline your actions to achieve your goal. You may not know everything that you need to do at once, but having a detailed outline will help you stay on track and achieve your goal the way you want to. So, now you must write down all the things you need to do to achieve your goal.

5. ***Omit the things that don't align with your schedule.*** The omission of unimportant things in your plan towards your goal is vital. Often in your day, there will be many things that are not aligned with your goal but take up a lot of time. For such activities, you need to understand how to remove them from your daily routine so that you can make time for the things that matter. Yes, some things like giving time to your family or going for a workout in the morning matter because they are essential parts of your life, and you don't need to omit them. However, it would be best to stop wasting time on social media or other useless activities to make time for the things that matter. When you are to take action, you should try your best

to not do the things that don't matter and entirely focus on the things that do matter. This deep focus will help you to achieve your goal quickly and fulfill your passion.

It would be best if you planned out your actions this way. Remember, clarity is the key. Ambiguity, unclearness, or confusion in your plan will not help but instead trouble you with deciding what it is that you need to do. Remember, if you let all of these doubtful and confusing things rise through your plan and there is a lack of crystal-clear clarity, you will always get confused, and instead of making a burger with lettuce, you will stuff it with cheese! Beware of ambiguity!

Part Three

Dream.

Believe.

Achieve.

8

The Power of Belief

Knowing your passion and goal has helped you find meaning and purpose in life, and now it is time to spring into action! Doing this should be simple because we have already discussed how to plan and set goals the right way. But no matter how righteously you set the goals and how properly you plan, you will not be able to take concrete and proper actions without a critical component: self-belief. Without self-belief, you will always be afraid of taking action and facing new challenges, and therefore having belief in yourself plays a pivotal role in achieving your goals.

But before that, we need to understand what a belief is and how it works. After that, we will be well equipped to understand its implementation in our life to accelerate our way to success. A belief is something that we consider to be true and use to direct our lives. Whatever we believe in is right for us and whatever is opposite to our beliefs is what we don't hold to be true. One of the most common beliefs that we have in today's world is countries. Everyone believes that countries exist, and if someone said that countries don't exist, we would consider them to be a liar. However, if we remove all the country borders and names, then countries don't exist. What truly exists is the large landmass that spans across the earth. Now, we can say that countries' existence is a belief that binds all of us together across the world. Therefore, we need to understand the difference between universal truths and beliefs.

A universal truth is something universally true. Everyone knows that mountains, beaches, and cities exist in today's world. Everyone knows that water exists. Everyone knows that giraffes have long necks and that hens lay eggs. These are universal truths, and we can't change them. However, beliefs are a little different from the realities. Remember the definition of belief that says, "A belief is something that we consider to be true."

Here is the catch! Since a belief is something that "we consider" to be true, it doesn't need to be a truth. For example, many people in today's world read eBooks, while some others still prefer paperbacks. When we ask the person who likes paperback books why he/she does so, the most common answer is, "Reading eBooks is not fun at all. When you read with a physical book in your hand, the reading experience becomes completely different." That's a belief and not a truth. Why? Because actually, the content of an eBook and a real book is not different at all. It is only the book's presentation, which makes the difference, and it is not a lot. The format of the book does not change the content you consume. Therefore, this statement is not a truth but a belief.

You may be wondering— what is the importance of beliefs in success and happiness, anyway? Well, that is quite important, and we will understand it once we know how beliefs work. When you believe in something, you consider it to be true. You have confidence in that particular belief, and because of that, it is right for you. However, beliefs are not universal truths, and that is why they change.

Take this example. Mike recently started shopping on a new e-commerce website, and the company's massive discounts made Mike believe that it was the best. He recommended this site to all of his friends, and they were happy too. But Mike noticed something strange. He started getting emails from new mailing lists he did not even know. He spoke to his friends about it, and they told him that they were also receiving unknown emails from new lists. Mike thought over this problem and was frustrated with seeing his inbox filled up with unnecessary emails. Finally, Mike realized that the source of this problem was the e-commerce company offering goods at a massive discount. The company was selling the email ids of its customers to other companies, which caused the problem. Mike immediately closed his account and unsubscribed from all those mailing lists at once. With this one event, Mike changed his belief in the company being the best, and he started thinking quite the opposite.

Beliefs help us this way. Whatever views we have about ourselves or our lives are what we consider accurate, and because we think these beliefs to be true, they become real for us. How so? Let's understand.

When you believe in something, your mind considers it to be correct, and therefore you act that way. Go back to when you were in the early years of schooling. Think about the classroom walls, your little friends, the teacher, the furniture, and form a picture of your classroom. Now, imagine that the teacher calls you and says, "You have done a great job. You are a star, and you will shine bright!" You are happy, and you go back to your table. Next, the teacher calls on another student and says, "You have not done a great job at all! You messed up everything, and you really won't be able to do much in life! Mark my words!" This child feels down and sullen with fear and grief. He thinks that he is worth nothing and the teacher is right. This belief gets instilled in his mind.

Fast forward twenty-five years, and both of you

have now passed out from college and are working professionals. You have become the CEO of a young tech start-up, and you happen to interview someone for the position of a base-level employee. The person you are interviewing is your friend from early school, and you identify him by his name.

His shoulders are drooped, his chin downwards, an uncomfortable and unnatural smile on his face, and an underconfident body language. You cannot believe that you were studying with this person once and now you are interviewing him for a base-level job. You don't let your bias towards him come in, and after the interview, you have no choice but to reject him because you could not see the confidence and the enthusiasm you were seeking for an employee at this position.

You remember the day when the teacher praised you and insulted him, and you realize that it was this belief that made a lot of difference.

The boy who was insulted thought that the teacher was right and made her words his belief. He had the choice to dismiss her words and believe that he was capable, but he accepted the negative sentiment, and because he considered it to be accurate, it became real.

This is the power of belief. Whatever you consider being true becomes true. No matter whatever your beliefs may be, they will become true for you. Beliefs can make or break a person; it is only up to the person to decide what kinds of beliefs they want to instill and accept.

9

Self-belief: The Driving Force for Success

Now that we have understood what the word belief means, we need to understand what self-belief is and how it works. Self-belief will allow us to be fully confident of ourselves and achieve our goals by taking well-planned and meaningful action. Yes, we can take action without self-belief, but we will doubt and not give out our fullest potential. Self-belief plays a vital role in our success and fulfillment; let's understand how.

First of all, we need to combine the words 'self' and 'belief' to understand what self-belief truly means. The dictionary meaning of self-belief on collinsdictionary.com is, ***"Self-belief is confidence in your own abilities or judgment."***

This definition is very self-explanatory and

accurate. Self-belief means having confidence in your ability to do anything you want. Having this sense of belief and faith in yourself will allow you to take risks, get over self-doubt and fear, shine bright by fulfilling your passion, and stay on track.

One of the biggest questions that people have is, "How do I develop self-belief?" And the answer to this is very simple and straightforward. You first need to understand how your foundational beliefs and thoughts developed in the first place, and we will use that to form the beliefs that empower us.

Your thoughts define your world. Whatever you feed to your mind, it accepts. Self-belief and other beliefs form when the mind soaks them in and lets them grow. Just like a loaf of bread makes you feel satiated and fulfills your body, your thoughts fulfill your mind. Whatever you feed to your body eventually decides how it will turn out in the future, and whatever you provide to your mind right now will ultimately determine how you turn out to be in the future. Your thoughts define your mindset, belief, confidence, and finally, your life.

Earl Nightingale has beautifully summarized the working of the mind in the following words, **"I want to tell you about a situation that parallels the human mind. Suppose a farmer has some land and it's good fertile land. Now the land gives the farmer a choice. He may plant in that land whatever he** chooses. The land doesn't care. It's up to the farmer to make the decision. Now, remember, we're comparing the human mind with the land because the mind, like the land, doesn't care what you plant in it. It will return what you plant but it doesn't care what you plant. Now let's say that the farmer has two seeds in his hand. One is a seed of corn, the other is nightshade, a deadly poison. He digs two little holes in the earth and he plants both seeds, one corn, the other nightshade. He covers up the holes, waters and takes care of the land, and what will happen? Invariably, the land will return what's planted. As it's written in the Bible, "As ye sow, so shall ye reap." Now, remember, the land doesn't care. It'll return poison in just as wonderful abundance as it will corn, so up come the two plants, one corn, one poison. The human mind is far more fertile, far more incredible and mysterious than the land, but it works the same way. It doesn't care what we plant, success, failure. A concrete, worthwhile goal, or confusion. Misunderstanding, fear, anxiety, and so on. But what we plant, it must return to us."

These lines contain profound meaning, and by understanding them, we will realize how self-belief works. You may be wondering, why does the mind accept everything that we give to it? Why doesn't it reject the wrong things and allow the right things to prosper? Let's find the answer!

The human mind has limited energy in a day, and it takes a lot of energy to analyze and process each of the thousands of thoughts that we have. Therefore, the mind is always looking for ways to conserve energy and use the least amount of energy to process a thought. When the mind tries to do this, it goes for the automation of behaviors and beliefs that occur repeatedly. If you continuously say to yourself, "I am an idiot!" at first, the mind will process this. Still, when it notices constant repetition of this thought, it will simply mark it and say, "Okay! Enough! You are an idiot!" which will then become a belief that you carry.

All of the things we think of are like seeds for the mind's fertile garden. As we discussed in the previous paragraph, the mind has thousands of things to analyze. That is why it cannot find time to classify and differentiate between good or bad and negative or positive. Only when we are conscious can we classify something as right or wrong. That's why the mind will return whatever it is that we plant. The mind is always taking in these seeds, and when they are nurtured through repetition, supporting actions, and indulgence in similar kinds of content, they soon turn into bigger plants. As we know, the mind does not classify anything as right or wrong— it just soaks everything in and allows whatever it is that you are giving it to grow. That is why you may find that some people are very keen at finding out the fault in other people because they have dropped and nurtured the seed of pin-pointing and gossiping in their heads. However, many people give appreciation and constructive feedback to others because they cultivate and grow the seeds of positivity and gratitude. Whatever you plant inside comes outside of you.

Just like your money compounds over and over with the right investment decisions, the positive and confident feed also compounds exponentially in your mind, giving you results on similar lines. However, just like your bodyweight compounds and grows as you eat unhealthily, the negative and fearful feed you give to your mind compounds and makes you a nervous and pessimistic person. As Earl Nightingale has rightly said, "We become what we think about."

Choosing your thoughts the right way matters. We need to select the kind of thoughts that align with our goal so that our minds can develop and grow on them and give us the plant of self-belief and confidence. Whatever you think about frequently is what you will attract in your life!

Your self-belief determines your life's trajectory since, with every impromptu thought that is related to your goal, you are paving the way for yourself. However, with every negative spontaneous thought, you are only destroying the road you paved for yourself. With every negative thought, you are destroying your thoughts' positive compounding, and with every positive thought, you are destroying the compounding of your negative thoughts. You choose and decide which thought you would allow compounding and which ones you will destroy.

10

How Your Initial Beliefs Determine the Trajectory of Your Life

Foundational beliefs are one of the most necessary parts of a person's life because they determine the outlook someone has towards their lives. A set of foundational beliefs is important because, without them, you would have no idea of how to take action and see if something is good or bad for you personally. Often, the foundational beliefs form in childhood, and that is why parents need to create a positive environment for their children at home. Let's see how foundational beliefs form and how they transform the life that a person leads.

A newborn baby is like a blank hard drive on your new computer. It hardly has any data on it. As you use your computer, you download files, give it data, use applications, and fill your hard drive with a lot of information. With each application you download, there are thousands and thousands of small files that you can't even count. Your computer's hard drive fills with data you either don't remember or are worried about deleting because you don't know how it came on your hard drive. Your hard drive now has some data that will permanently be there, and you don't want to erase it.

Similarly, when you are born, there is hardly any data in you except for knowing who your mother is. As you grow through your infancy and childhood, you observe everything very keenly and without judgment because you still do not have any founding beliefs surrounding your life. Just like you download files and applications on your computer, a child's mind also downloads beliefs and thought processes from its surroundings. If some of those things repeat, again and again, they turn into foundational beliefs.

Whatever you plant, you will get, which is why a child's foundational beliefs are so important. When a young child is growing, the first seeds of thought planted are like the first crop on soil that no one has used before. If you buy a fresh piece of land and plant wheat on it, the plant will successfully grow, and if you plant wheat again and again over the years, this becomes the dominant plant in the area, and the wheat changes the soil to support its growth. In the same way, when the surroundings sow the seeds of a particular plant in a child's mind, they grow there successfully, and if planted, again and again, they change the soil of the mind to support their growth and become beliefs.

Therefore, having a nearly constant positive environment can give the child a chance to flower. An almost endless negative environment can give the child only the strength to succumb to circumstances. Children's minds accept everything that goes in because there is nothing to be classified, and that is why the child is always curious and uses the first set of thoughts to form the foundational beliefs.

Therefore, there are some timid and under-confident students in the same schools and localities, along with very confident and outgoing students. The significant difference in their approach towards life is decided by their upbringing at home when they were young. Let's take the example of two six-year-old kids studying at the same school and living in the same area in Downtown New York. Their school and locality were the same, but was there any real difference in their upbringing? Let's see.

The first kid, Joe, was raised by his mom and grandmother because his father left his family very soon after his birth. He did not remember what his father looked like, but he was happy because his home environment was encouraging and positive. His grandmother would always pick him up from school, take him to the park, play with him, talk to him, teach him good habits by giving him rewards and letting him eat his favorite foods on weekends. She taught him the importance of healthy food through a story, so he started eating healthy food. In the evening, when his mom returned from her job, she would give all of her time to him, and he would feel happy. His mom and grandmother did not scold him but taught him the lesson politely when he made mistakes, and he was practically explained and told the importance of doing and not doing some things.

Joe received this kind of upbringing, even though his family fell apart very early, and he never had the support of his dad.

However, for the second kid, Samuel, things were a little different. He was born at about the same time as Joe, and both studied in the same class. Joe and Samuel were good friends and always played together. At home, however, Samuel was not given love, attention, and positivity. His parents forced him to get up early in the morning and eat a cold sandwich for lunch after returning from school. He also had to make sure that he locked the doors, no one was inside and never played with the electricity. He had both his mom and dad, but they spent most of their time in a job and the rest of it fighting about money without reaching any conclusions, as his mother would go back to look after dinner, and his dad would go back to watch the television. No one would look up to Samuel and care for how he felt. They would think that everything was fine until he started crying and was either given food or a milk bottle to spend his time on. If that did not work, he got a toy that made him happy at the moment, and then his parents would get back to other tasks.

He did not get enough attention from his parents. They planted the seeds of not paying attention to other people, fighting without finding solutions, and living negatively in him. The lack of attention that his parents gave him made him unconsciously think that he was not good enough, and therefore he unconsciously started making a mess and then cried and complained a lot to get their attention. He did not want to create a mess or disturbance for his parents, but the thought that he was not good enough made him underconfident in almost everything. That's why when he made a mistake, he felt as if he had done something wrong and would start crying. When he did that, his parents would get mad at him and scold him very badly. Whenever he repeated a mistake or made a new one and started crying, his parents made remarks regarding him that negatively influenced his mindset. All of the negative comments about him not being good got deeply embedded in his attitude. As he grew, the negative foundational beliefs made him a very different person than Joe, who did not have the privilege of a father but had positive foundational beliefs. Both of them saw the world through their foundational beliefs, and their lives turned out to be different because one could only see problems, but the other always came up with solutions.

We talked about how a person's foundational beliefs determined their life trajectory and discussed how the effect is powerful and profound. Yes, a person can change their foundational beliefs, but it takes a lot of effort to unlearn and relearn completely. If a person does not do that, then the negative foundational beliefs can give rise to two obstacles— fear and self-doubt— which can block the path towards success and fulfillment.

11

Fear: The First Obstacle to Success and Fulfillment

"There is only one thing that makes a dream impossible to achieve: the fear of failure."

—Paulo Coelho, The Alchemist

Three years ago, I was traveling with my dad at night. We stopped at a road crossing to turn towards our house. And then, I felt a sudden jerk, and everything went blank. It all happened within a split second, and for some moments after that, a tormentingly fearful state of mind took away my awareness, leaving me blank. I saw everything around me, but I don't remember anything, and that experience of the blankness of some seconds embedded deep into my mind. Soon, I opened my eyes and saw our car in front of a truck, when it was behind a car a few moments ago. I was bewildered, and I did not know what was happening. There was a sudden shock, and I remember my body feeling a jerk, but I did not realize that it was a car crash until I got out and saw the havoc.

 I was hurt on my left leg, and blood dripped as I got out of my car and saw three cars wrecked in the middle of a road crossing, with a traffic jam developing near the crash site. A pick-up truck hit our car from the back, and then it crashed ahead. There was chaos as people frantically scurried around, and the traffic tried finding its way through the wreck. I was utterly confused until I finally calmed myself down and reached home. At home, I got my injury treated, and then I went to sleep that night.

 That night, I experienced the scariest thing I ever faced in my entire life, as that blankness made me feel fearful. I did not and still do not want to experience anything like that.

After this experience, that road crossing and the turn towards my home became a dark memory for me, and I feared it. The next day I did not go to school, but I went the day after. My school bus used to go right through that crossing in that busy road every morning. After two days, I still saw pieces of glass and headlights lying in the road crossing when I went to school. The crash's fresh memories flashed through my mind; I became fearful and started having negative thoughts about a car crash. I went to school day in and day out, but this fear persisted, and I didn't even consciously think that I was fearful of this road crossing.

Finally, a month or so after the crash, we got our car repaired, and it returned. When I traveled in it the next time, and as we passed through the crossing, I felt fearful again and looked a little here and there, especially at the back, to make sure that no car was behind us. For the next few months, I grew to be very fearful of this particular section on the road. I always looked at the back and wanted dad to drive out of this section as quickly as possible. Sometimes, we would have to wait for the traffic to pass by, and the fear would grip me again, making me look around. I did not want to relive that scene, and that is why I became fearful of it.

I became fearful of the crossing, but I had to understand how to overcome this negative feeling. To do this, I had to go to the deep, core meaning of the word 'fear' and understand the reasons behind its upheaval to find a way out of this pessimistic turmoil. In the remainder of this chapter, we will be discussing how to do that.

What is fear? If I were to ask you this question, what would your answer be? It may be something on these lines, "Fear is being afraid or scared of something," which is the typical image of fear that we have in our mind, and it is partly correct because fear does involve a sense of being scared. If I were to ask you, "What does it mean to be afraid or scared?" You may say, "It means to be fearful of something." We have just come back to where we started, and this whole loop of being afraid meaning fearful, and fear meaning being afraid, is something that won't lead us anywhere. A more thoughtful meaning of being afraid is, "It is feeling unsure and uncertain of what is going to happen ahead, and that is bringing about anxiety and a feeling of worry." Fear is the uncertainty of the future.

When is it that you feel the most fearful? It isn't when you are going from your home to the local grocery store. But will you feel afraid of doing the same thing when no one is around, and it is completely dark? The answer is yes, but why? Because the silence and the darkness create a sense of suspense and anxiety about what lies ahead. Fear doesn't only come up when you feel unsure of what lies ahead of you. Fear also arises when you are in a situation that turned out badly for you in the past, and you start to worry if the same thing will happen to you in the present. Whenever I traveled through that road crossing again, I felt fearful because I anticipated and worried about the chances of suffering from the pain of a car crash again. Fear also comes up when you are on the verge of making a crucial decision in your life because you don't know what the result of this decision will be.

We think that fear is an uncontrollable emotion that arises when we are at the point of uncertainty. But actually, there is a way out of this emotion because fear is nothing but a state of mind like happiness, sadness, joy, etc. Like all other different states of mind, fear is also under our control. External factors affect fear, but only for a temporary amount of time, which we can control from the inside. The external factors can be anything like a sudden shock or the happening of a particular event you never expected. Still, over time, it will be upon you how you choose to react to these fears, and this is what makes fear controllable.

Fear has been a part of human psychology from primitive times. In the world today, a sense of fear, insecurity, and worry affects us negatively, limiting our capabilities. But actually, fear did not negatively affect the primitive hunter-gatherers or in the same manner that it affects us today. Fear helped the human race survive and flourish through various millennia of rapid change and evolution. Without fear, we would not have survived as a species, getting wiped out thousands of years ago. Fear aided early humans in deciding on the best response, which guaranteed the highest chance of survival in any situation. We must thank our ancestors because we might not have existed without their creative use of fear!

In any situation that came across, every animal and human had to choose one of any three survival responses: fight, flight, and freeze, which the humans and animals decided based on fear. Let's see how fear played out this vital role. The humans knew that lions were dangerous carnivores, and that is why when they saw one, they chose the flight response out of the fear of being eaten up and ran away to save themselves. The humans knew that giraffes wouldn't do anything to them, so they fearlessly chose the freeze mode by quickly strolling past them or staying next to them. But, when the humans saw another tribe of humans trying to enter their area, they felt fearful of losing their food source and chose the option of fighting to defend their land.

Most of us don't realize this, but early humans' three survival techniques are fundamental in our present life. The only difference is that we don't have to worry about lions chasing us down the plains or another tribe attacking our tribe. We have much more complex issues, but we still use these three responses in our everyday life to prioritize our actions and increase our chances of survival.

What if humans did not have any fear in them and were utterly fearless? Well, if there was no fear, then primitive humans would have suffered a lot from lack of correct judgment and would then turn out to be the most cognitively unevolved animals. Because without fear, early humans would have miserably mixed and matched how they chose the three responses. If there was no fear, early humans might have chosen to freeze in front of lions, and we all know what the result would have been. Early humans might have decided to flee from a neighboring tribe if there was no fear, making them lose their land and food source. And, worst, of course, the early humans might have chosen to fight with the harmless giraffes, and I believe that seldom would these people return without any broken bones. The damage that lack of fear would have caused is evident, and if it had continued this way, then our species would have gone extinct because of making poor decisions and getting killed more often.

In the same way, fear helps us today by allowing us to judge a scenario and choose the right response. For example, we stop at the red-light during traffic and choose the freeze mode to save ourselves from a collision. If this kind of fear didn't exist, we would not have successfully implemented safety rules and saved lives by reducing traffic collisions. That is why fear is essential and beneficial to us— it increases our chances of survival. These kinds of fears are known as biological fears and must be present in everyone to guarantee survival. But when we use our cognitive abilities a little more to anticipate the future, we create unnecessary concerns that negatively impact us. These are known as psychological fears because they exist only in our heads and don't play any vital role in our survival; therefore, we should get rid of them.

Now that we know what fear is and how it arises, we must understand how to overcome it. You may be having multiple fears, and knowing which ones are psychological and which ones biological, is very important. The fear of darkness or the fear of taking some risk is psychological as we create it, but the fear of falling off a cliff or falling from a tall building is biological.

That is why you must think consciously over the fear you are trying to overcome. When you can mark a clear distinction between the biological and psychological fears that you have, you will keep the necessary fears for survival while getting rid of the limiting ones by following the steps below.

1. ***Calm yourself down.*** Often when the fearful state of mind is present, you are not calm and continuously thinking about what might happen and what might not. So, the best thing to do is simply calm yourself down and let the fearful state subside. The most effective way of doing this is just closing your eyes, taking in deep, calm breaths, and merely focusing on them. Allow all thoughts to come to your mind but don't concentrate on any. This small exercise will help you get back in the present and put you in a rational state for self-reflection.

2. ***Listen to whatever is going on inside of you.*** One of the very first things that you

need to do is listen to yourself. Often in the hustle and bustle of life, we forget to listen to whatever is going on inside us, and that is what you need to do. You need to recognize your fears. Often, we don't know why and even what we precisely fear in a particular situation until we look deep into ourselves and understand our concerns. Don't hate your fears; instead, simply listen to them. Even an extremely agitated person will calm down if they get a listening ear, and that is what you need to do with your fears. You need to be the listening ear and a faithful companion to them. Your worries will open up, and you will know what it is that you are fearing.

Now, some people may say that their fear is evident to them. Maybe it is the neighbor's dog or bungee jumping. The dog or the activity is just a substitute for the real fear in the material world. The dog and the activity are just the veils and the clothes that your fear is wearing. To truly understand the fear, you need to tug away these clothes and covers to see the fear's true essence. Here is how you can do that. When you listen to yourself and examine your concerns, you should first let all of the chatter inside of you subside. Sit down, and let thoughts come as they come— just patiently wait and sit.

At one point, the thoughts will go away, and you would have technically finished the act of listening, but the process doesn't end there. Once all of your drivel and chatter has silenced itself, get into the process of asking questions. You need to be a master interrogator trying to crack a case by inter-rogating the criminals (that are your fears in this case). So, you have to consider what you are fearful about, ask the reason behind it, and continue asking why until the real truth uncovers.

So, if I take my example of fearing the road crossing after the crash, I would have done an interrogation the following way, "Why am I feeling fearful of that crossing?" The answer would be, "Because I don't want to get involved in a car crash again." The next follow-up question would be, "Why do I not want to get involved in a car crash?" These questions may sound obvious, but it is es-sential to ask them to get to your real fear. I would reply to this question in this man-ner— "I don't want to be involved in a car crash again because I know how bad it is as I have experienced this before." The next question will be, "Why is it bad?" The an-swer, "Because it is painful and chaotic." Another follow-up question can be, "Why is it painful and chaotic?" The answer,

"Because car accidents are never pleasant. They always hurt people and also kill them." Another question will be, "Why do I want to avoid pain and chaos?" My answer would be, "Because I want to be orderly, and I want to have control of my life." The next question would again be, "So, why do I fear a car crash?" Now, my final answer would be, "I fear a car crash because I don't want to face chaos and pain in the same way that I did before."

In the same way, you will be able to break everything down and find your core fear. My fear was the fear of suffering the same way I did in the past. When I was in the same location where I had the previous car crash, I felt fearful because all the pain and chaos swept through my mind, making me wonder if it would return. In the same way, you also need to pull off each layer and see the truth behind the veils of your fear.

3. ***Think about your actions.*** Once you have control over your fearful state, and you know your real fear, you can easily use the circumstances to understand what triggers those feelings. It is imperative to know your fear's true nature to make sure that you can overcome it. If you fear a dog in your vicinity, you don't fear the dog as a

creature— you fear the pain it will cause when it bites. Otherwise, it looks charming and adorable.

As we learned before, the mind has limited storage, and it tries to automate as many things as possible. When you are fearful of something, the mind notices the true nature of fear and the circumstances created around it. Every time the mind can't analyze the situation and say, "Okay! Now I am in the same place that I was four days ago, and I saw the same dog with big, fiery teeth going past me making me fearful, and now I must feel fearful again." The mind does not have the time or energy to conduct such an analysis, so it merely finds a behavior or action that will automatically produce a response— feeling fearful— when triggered. Continuing with the example of your neighbor's dog, you will realize that the trigger of your fear is the dog's presence near you. You don't feel fear when the dog is behind the gate or on the balcony, but you feel fearful when taking a stroll out on the road. So, the fear makes an image in your mind, and when something pulls the trigger, the fear strikes, and the pre-conceived notion that you have of the dog comes up and makes you fearful.

With this understanding, you can now start to use the trigger to help you feel differently by associating a new picture with the stimulus.

In the case of the dog's example, you can use the same trigger to form a completely different image by imagining that dog coming towards you with affection as you pick it up to hold it with love and joy. Changing the impression that you associate with the trigger is one of the most effective ways of overcoming fear as you are reprogramming your mind to think differently.

Let's consider bungee jumping. If you fear bungee jumping, then simply imagine yourself rolling across the line, feeling the rush of adrenaline and a sense of adventure, instead of the anxiety of falling. This way, you will associate a positive picture with bungee jumping, and you will overcome your fear. By deliberately practicing this, again and again, your mind will become immensely accustomed to this new way of thinking, and the new responses will automatically arise when your mind gets the old triggers.

4. ***Imagine the worst that can happen.*** There are often many people who are fearful of certain things, and when they realize the true essence of their fears, it usually

boils down to three significant fears: the fear of failure, the fear of suffering, and the fear of being judged. These three significant fears also narrow down to one thing— the uncertainty of the future. When you had a painful experience, and the current situation is similar, you feel fearful. When you do something new, you don't know what people may be feeling about you, and you don't know what the future may have in store for you, which makes you feel fearful.

In all of these cases, the first thing that needs to be done by you is to calm yourself down. When you are in a calm state, imagine the worst thing that can happen due to your fear. I also overcame my fear of car accidents on that particular crossing this way. So, I deconstructed my fear to its final essence, which was to avoid pain and suffering. Now, I imagined my fear, and I thought of the worst thing that may happen to me. It came out to be that in the worst-case scenario, I could die. It is as simple as that. I felt a completely different change in my perspective, and I was like, "Yes if the worst thing ever happens, I will most probably die." And that was all the realization I needed. I did not need to know anything else. All of it ended here, and with it, my fear went away. Why so? Because I came to know that I will die one day or another, but

I don't need to waste my precious time worrying about dying.

When you fully concentrate on this, you will realize that no consequence is worse than death, and most probably, this won't be the consequence in your scenario, and even if it is—just like it was in mine—you will still know of it, and you will proceed with full care. You will live in the moment instead of fear. You will realize that you were overthinking, and your fear will go away. If you fear trying out a new business model, and even after knowing that the worst thing happening to you will be losing all your money and declaring bankruptcy, you are still fearful. The best thing for you to do is try out whatever you fear on a small scale and see if it fails or works. If it works, then great, and if it doesn't, you have still gained some experience. You can do this with any psychological fear. Try it out for yourself, and it will help you to understand and overcome your fears.

By overcoming your fears, you have gained one of the most important things you need to develop confidence and self-belief: fearlessness. This fearlessness doesn't mean irresponsible behavior and actions. This fearlessness means keeping all the necessary survival instincts in mind and not letting the unnecessary side of fear take over you and prevent you from making the right decisions just because you were uncertain.

12

Self-doubt: The Final Obstacle

You have now overcome half of the obstacles in your journey towards confidence and self-belief. Now that half the battle is won, all you need to do is get over the last barrier— self-doubt— and win this battle against your limiting beliefs.

Self-doubt makes people doubt their capabilities because they become uncertain of what may lie ahead and don't initiate any actions out of fear. This trait makes you live in fear and uncertainty, but if you are the kind of person who wants to live a truly fulfilling and happy life to achieve your goals and believe in yourself, you need to get over self-doubt and take bold actions. Here's how.

Before understanding how to overcome self-doubt, you need to know why self-doubt comes up in the first place. Well, it is merely because of the image you have of yourself, and this quotation by Charles Horton Cooley beautifully expresses how this image is formed, **"I am not what I think I am, and I am not what you think I am. I am what I think you think I am."**

Let's understand this line carefully. It says that you are not what you think of yourself, and you are also not what others think of you, but you are the person you think you are in the eyes of others. It is the perception you have about how others feel about you. You are forming an identity of yourself that you perceive to be existing in others' eyes. Many people act on this basis, thinking that this is the way people see them, and hence they must work in this way only to shine and succeed. Well, having this kind of perception is far from reality, and trying to behave and act in this way to seek social approval and success is what whips up self-doubt.

Why is taking actions based on perceptions wrong? Well, first of all, it is because forming an extensive image of yours takes time and is a vital process. But when you do it on the mere basis of speculation, it is like playing with fire. Opinions change rapidly, and therefore if you try to maintain your identity based on them, you will land up in a whirlpool of identities where you won't know who you truly are. Your true identity doesn't change, but the way you form one for yourself can change rapidly.

Handling such uncertainty can be difficult; thus, you try to stick to an identity accepted in society. You try sticking to this "untrue" identity just for the sake of fitting in. You doubt yourself and your capabilities when you try to go out of this image you have formed for yourself. You try breaking out, and it seems complicated, and you decide not to take any substantial action as you are unsure of losing your speculation-based identity.

To truly achieve success, you need to overcome this self-doubt. You must understand your true self so that you can shatter this old, limiting identity and shine bright with confidence and self-belief.

As a result of self-doubt, another very destructive trait that arises is the inferiority complex. First coined by psychologist Alfred Adler in 1907, people have researched this concept and discussed it in psychology. When you doubt your capabilities and think that you can't achieve or do something with your life, you start to think about being inferior and inadequate compared to other people. An inferiority complex is a feeling of lack, inadequacy, and mediocrity arising from reality or imagined insecurity. The root cause for the development of the inferiority complex is comparing yourself to others and believing that you are below and less successful or sadder than those around you, making you feel insecure about making it out in the world. Through this kind of pessimistic comparison, you destroy your self-belief profoundly. That's why you need to know how to overcome self-doubt and get over the inferiority complexes you may have.

To change how you think of yourself, eradicate self-doubt, and form a new identity, you need to go through each of these steps and implement them to embark on this journey of self-discovery and identification: –

1. ***Acknowledge and understand your real self.*** Your authentic self hides behind the veil of the image you have created based on what you think people feel about you. Therefore, all you need to do is lift this veil and uncover the real self. The simplest way to do this is by questioning and reflecting. Take a sheet of paper and write on it everything that you think of yourself. You don't need to judge or classify anything at this point; all you need to do is write down every possible thing you can think of about yourself. Then, go through your list again and see how perceptions shape many things about you. It would be best if you did the classification now, and you can do it in any

way you want. Go through the things you have written down, and from there, pick up each item, look at it deeply and think if this thing is you. You need to ask yourself and understand how factual those statements are.

For example, you write down that you are overweight. The reason for you to think this way maybe that your friends told you to eat more healthily or your mom told you that the jeans you bought a couple of years ago don't fit you anymore. Now, you have formed an identity with being overweight. Your mom and friends indirectly said these things to you, but what you derived from them mattered the most as it created your identity. That is why Charles Horton Cooley was correct about image formation. You did not form an identity for yourself with what you thought, and neither did you create an identity with what others thought about you. But you did make an identity by perceiving and believing what others might be thinking about you.

No one said you were overweight, but you derived this meaning from how you looked at the statements. To understand the depth of identity formation, let's explore the various aspects that you can derive from this statement in the way that Charles Horton

Cooley describes. Your friends tell you that you should eat more healthily. The various ways in which you can see this thing are:

a. Your friends think you are already in good shape and should eat more healthily to avoid weight gain.

b. Maybe your friends are mocking you for eating junk food once or twice and that you won't be affected much by it.

c. You are fit, but you have started gaining weight. That's why your friends are giving you the warning to curb this little weight gain before it is too late.

We have derived three different meanings from a single statement, and the question is: can a person be these many things? No, right? But, then, can one opinion have so many different connotations? Well, it is merely because the statement isn't the truth. If one statement can have so many different conclusions, then how can we say it is true? We know that Newton's Law of Gravity is true, and it exists because we can't draw out multiple conclusions from this theory. We don't say that gravity is the force of attraction between two celestial objects that also repels and pushes back the objects when they are too close to avoid a collision. This sounds very absurd, right? It seems logical to derive many different kinds of opinions from your friends' statement, but does it seem logical to do that with Newton's law? I don't think so.

Maybe you realize that your body is going through a growth phase right now, so your jeans have become short, and you are eating more and more. Your body shape isn't becoming broader in terms of fat, so you realize that you aren't overweight. Both your mom's and your friends' statements did not hold or make up for your identity. When you slam the facts right into the face of ambiguity and false perceptions, you realize the substantial truth of your current state.

When you go through this exercise and keep checking off things you thought were true but were simply perceptions that you had, you will realize the real truth about yourself and how it affects your thoughts and feelings. This way, you need to reflect upon each thing on your list and determine if these things are real or just perceptions. You figure out who your authentic self is, and you will acknowledge and understand it. Thus, all your perceptions will go away, and the truth will lie right in front of you.

2. ***Think of areas for improvement in your real self.*** As you go through this

exercise, you will be cutting out all the misconceptions you had about yourself, and you will understand your authentic self. Now that you know this, you need to think of the areas in which you can improve your real self. You have already crossed the biggest hurdle in overcoming self-doubt, that is removing all misconceptions. Now, however, you need to find out places where you need to improve. You must keep in mind that whatever you are improving should be necessary for surviving in this world or related to your goal. It would be best if you did not spend time on unimportant things. When you find out what you need to improve on, you can make a goal statement and achieve it. It is essential to keep improving continually. Self-doubt is like weeds— it grows wherever it finds mediocrity and space. If you need to develop some skill related to your passion, you need to improve, because if you don't, your mediocrity may give rise to self-doubt, making you doubt your capabilities and destroying self-belief.

3. ***Change your perspective about yourself.*** When you do the exercise to find out who your real self is, you will gain great insights to lift the veil of identities that you have formed based on misconceptions. All you need to do is slowly drop all

the judgments and perceptions while embracing who you indeed are. When you accept your reality, you realize that your potential is infinite, and this one belief will help you get over self-doubt very quickly.

Remember, the way you look at yourself defines your limits and capabilities, and you have the power to change this to your liking.

This way, you will be able to get over self-doubt and fear. Once you get over these two main obstacles, you will believe in yourself and have the confidence to do anything. When you have your goal in mind and get over these obstacles, you become genuinely limitless and capable of achieving anything!

13

Developing Self-Belief

Self-belief, as we discussed in Chapter Nine, is something we can develop and instill. The foundational beliefs that we have determine our outlook towards life, but it is still upto us if we want to allow the negative beliefs of fear, self-doubt, and pessimism to control our lives or not. Like all the other beliefs, we can change these negative beliefs, but only when we put in persistent efforts and dedication.

Foundational beliefs are like the thousands of files on a hard drive. To get a clean and clear hard drive like the one you had when you bought a new computer, you need to go through every file, see if it is essential and delete the rest. When you do this, you will have a nearly clean hard drive. Similarly, you need to put in the persistent effort to give your hundred percent and note down every belief you have. You must take this first step to develop a new sense of confidence and belief in achieving your goal. It may take time, but make sure that you write almost everything you think about yourself now and the beliefs you have about yourself. You can even start from the list you made when overcoming self-doubt and add thoughts to it as you have them. Like we did in the self-doubt exercise, you do not need to classify these thoughts and divide them. You just have to allow them to flow from your mind to the pen or the keyboard.

There is a straightforward reason for doing this exercise. When presented with information from outside, our conscious mind puts up a critical filter and assesses the knowledge before allowing it to enter. However, when we think about something on our own, the conscious mind does not filter these thoughts. Why? Because the conscious mind believes that these thoughts are a part of us, there is no need to analyze or critique them. That's where the purpose of this exercise kicks in. When you have written the beliefs and thoughts about yourself, you have externalized them. After writing, you need to distance yourself from these thoughts to divert yourself away from them.

After a sufficient time gap, you need to sit there and read the list out loud to yourself. When you do this, your conscious mind becomes aware and thinks that you are consuming some external content, and thus, it only allows the beliefs that match with the foundational beliefs to enter.

Let some time pass in between, and let these beliefs incubate and grow in your mind. After a long gap, maybe a few hours or a whole day, you need to revisit the list and this time, cut out the things you don't want to have in your life and keep the things you want. You should let your mind control this exercise as you mark the things as "Want" or "Don't Want."

When you have segregated the negative beliefs out, you need to think of the new, empowering beliefs that you want to instill and write them out on the same sheet. When you write down all of the new and empowering beliefs that help you achieve your goal, you engage multiple senses in the process. That creates much better concentration than just thinking, therefore allowing you to let the new beliefs embed deeply into your mind.

Now, you need to get the soil of your mind's fertile garden ready to receive the new crop of empowering beliefs. From the past many years, you may have had negative beliefs, and the soil of your mind would have changed accordingly to support the growth of negative beliefs. To make the new and positive beliefs a part of your life, you must plow the soil and regenerate it to make it suitable for a new crop type. You will get the ground ready for the new foundational beliefs that will change the soil accordingly and make you unstoppable.

To instill the new beliefs, you need to plant the seeds, nurture them, and let them grow into tall trees that dominate the soil of your mind. Here is how to do that and become confident and self-believing:

1. ***Think about the beliefs that you want to instill.*** Ralph Waldo Emerson said, **"A man is what he thinks about all day long."** You need to live by this statement to form good self-beliefs and gain confidence. When you are trying to achieve your goal, it is immensely vital for you to think about the goal and think about the empowering beliefs to achieve it. If you are not mentally prepared and determined to achieve your goal, you will not be able to do it. You need to bring in the determination by eradicating the negative beliefs and allowing the positive ones to prosper and grow. When you continuously think about something, it becomes your reality because that is what gets planted in your mind, and that is what you must do for positive beliefs!

2. ***Think the right way with affirmations!*** Remember, thinking itself won't do the job because thinking with the right emotion and feeling is also critical. Humans are emotional creatures, and

therefore we connect the most with things that have an emotion attached to them. Suppose you want to instill the belief that you are a great corporate trainer, and you say to yourself, "I am a great corporate trainer." You do this in an anxious, nervous, and worried tone. Do you think you will become a corporate trainer and let your mind take in this belief? The answer is no. It won't happen because the right emotion is not attached to it. If you were to say the same statement in an optimistic, energetic, and positive tone, the effect would be the opposite, and your mind will accept all the beliefs you put in.

The mind thinks only in the present tense and with emotional pictures, and that is why you must say and think about all of your beliefs in the present tense with a supporting emotion. That is why I stated the statement and the thought of becoming a great corporate trainer in the present tense in the above example. When you say and think about the beliefs that you want to instill with emotions and in the present tense, you are not just saying them, you are affirming them, and this kind of strong affirmation will help you plan and think about your beliefs in the right manner.

3. ***Take action.*** Just saying and saying and

thinking and thinking won't do because our mind is also intelligent enough to not believe everything at once. The mind accepts beliefs when you think about them the right way and instill them correctly, but the mind will also look at your present actions. If there is a significant difference between what you are saying and what you are doing, then the mind will conflict with which side to go to, and there will be no decision. However, if you take action and say these things to yourself, your present life and conscious thinking align to produce your mind's new beliefs' remarkable and exponential growth.

4. ***Repeat!*** Doing all of this once won't make a lot of difference, but doing all of these things consistently every day will naturally plow the soil of your mind, plant the new seeds and let them grow into positive and empowering beliefs. The soil will adapt to them to become the soil of positive beliefs, encouragement, and growth, which will boost your confidence and self-belief!

This way, you form the right beliefs, get over the ones that limit you, and truly become limitless. You will get yourself ready to embrace happiness, success, and fulfillment with the growth of the positive foundational beliefs that will rarely let any self-doubt or fear arise. And even if any of these two obstacles come up, you now have the tools to tackle them.

Thus, you will sculpt a beautiful garden whose soil hosts the plants that empower you to fulfill your fullest potential and achieve your goals. This path will lead you towards a truly fulfilling and meaningful life, and I know that you will pave it for yourself.

Part Four

Actions and

Habits

14

Taking Action

"The path to success is to take massive, determined actions."

—Tony Robbins

Congratulations! You have successfully made it to the last part of this book. Till now, you have learned about finding your passion, setting your goals, and understanding how belief works and determines your life's trajectory. Now, it is time to understand an essential part of your journey to living a meaningful life: taking action. Now is the time for real, concrete action, and once you understand how to take that, you will become truly unstoppable.

Taking action is very important because we would not achieve or do anything in our lives without any work. Without effort, there is nothing but only idea generation, which means that we will reap the most rewards and results when we take action. Therefore taking action as soon as possible would be one of the best things to do, right? Wrong. If you try to take any action without understanding, you are doing nothing else but competing with a monkey to see who can win the race of climbing a tree. You know that you will lose because you don't have any preparation and understanding, and no matter how hard you try, you will always meet disappointment. If you were to practice, understand, and learn how to climb trees properly, you might stand a chance at winning if the monkey is slow. In the race after training, you still lose, but the chances aren't 100 percent. Without any preparation and understanding, the chances of you losing are flat 100 percent. Therefore, no matter how quickly or later you start, your ability to get results through your actions will depend upon your understanding and planning efforts.

Thankfully, we have already done that by understanding our passion, planning the right way, and believing in ourselves. However, before launching into action, there are a few things that we need to understand to leverage our efforts properly to reap the best results.

Have you ever wondered why some people get so much done in less time while others spend their whole day and don't get many things done?

Let's understand both kinds of people through this example. The first person, Joseph, is a real estate agent in London and the second person, Marcus, is an accountant for a stockbroking firm in New York City. Joseph wakes up every day at six-thirty in the morning, spends around an hour on exercise, and then he gets ready for his office, has breakfast, and leaves at eight. On the other hand, Marcus wakes up at six-thirty as well and spends half an hour rolling around in bed until finally getting out at seven. Then he gets ready for his office in a haphazard manner, brews a cup of coffee, and eventually leaves his house with some money to buy a sandwich for breakfast on the way.

When Joseph travels in his car, he turns on his favorite song playlist, humming with happiness to his office. Meanwhile, Marcus is more worried about finding his favorite sandwich shop to be open and, if it isn't, then finding another restaurant for breakfast. He casually and inattentively listens to the radio news, shoving in all the negative that may be happening worldwide. Marcus often finds the shop closed on important days, and worriedly spends his time around the city trying to find the nearest breakfast spot. When he finds one, he quickly orders a sandwich with fries, takes it into the car, and starts munching on it while hurriedly driving to his office.

With both London and New York being crowded places, it becomes difficult to avoid traffic jams, and thus Marcus gets agitated when he has to get stuck in the rush hour, and while Joseph also has to do that, he does not lose his cool. Finally, both of them arrive at their offices around 9:30 AM, and their routine completely changes.

Joseph starts by opening up his calendar for the day, looking for the sites he needs to visit and what clients he needs to deal with today. He then spends the first half-hour planning out his time on his tasks for the day. On the other hand, Marcus opens up his laptop and documents, figuring out where he left yesterday, managing the company's trades and accounts. He does not have a plan, and he directly launches into action.

At ten o'clock, Joseph quickly grabs his car keys and goes to the first property to show it to a prospective buyer. He spends forty-five minutes there and comes back to the office at eleven. At that time, he goes for the weekly board meeting for an hour. Then, he quickly leaves to finish off the first deal of the day with a client, and after fifteen minutes, he does it. This way, he quickly finishes five deals by 1:30 PM and then goes for lunch. He eats in an up-scale restaurant because many wealthy people looking to buy some properties eat in these places. In the next half an hour of lunch, Joseph makes two more deals for the next day, and right from the restaurant, he goes to show a property to one of the buyers. Seeing that his next client's house for the day was also nearby, he did not go to the office but went straight to the buyer's home and finalized the sixth deal there, providing a personalized experience. At about three in the afternoon, Joseph is back at the office and takes another client for a property tour, finalizing another deal for the next day. At four, he comes back to the office, spends half an hour making his daily report of the work, and around 4:30 PM, he takes a cup of coffee and heads home.

In six hours of work, Joseph attended a board meeting, took three prospective buyers on a property tour, and finalized six deals, getting a lot of work done! Now let's see how Marcus spends his day. He starts working on an important sheet regarding a bulk deal when his colleague interrupts him and asks him to come for the board meeting scheduled at 10 AM. Marcus completely forgets about that and stops working to attend the board meeting. At 11:30 AM, he comes back, takes a break to check out his email and social media, and spends time on that until 12. He also has to finish the important sheet regarding a bulk deal when his friend invites him to join his group for lunch, and Marcus agrees. All of them simply gossip about multiple things and finish this break at 2 in the afternoon. Finally, Marcus wearily gets back to this enormous report. He works on it till seven in the evening, taking a coffee break of thirty minutes and checking his social media in between. In the end, Marcus is weary, has worked overtime, and has not finished his work either.

I guess it is evident that Joseph belongs to the productive category of people, while Marcus belongs to the other. Both wake up at 6:30 AM and reach the office simultaneously, but their emotional state, well-being, and productivity are the complete opposite and different. I am sure all of you want to be the "Joseph" in your work. To do that, you need healthy habits. To plan your day well and make it most productive with the right actions, you must have strong practices that support you and build you to help you achieve your goal on time. In the remainder of this section, we will be looking at just that!

15

What is a Habit?

"Man is largely a creature of habit, and many of his activities are more or less automatic reflexes from the stimuli of his environment."

—Granville Stanley Hall

Understanding habits and how they work is crucial in taking actions towards the right way for success. Various things go into habit formation, and understanding them will help us navigate through taking action until we achieve our goal.

Before stepping into habit formation, we must understand what a habit exactly is. Do you brush every day? Do you eat food every day? Do you travel to your school or office every day? Do you call someone from your cell phone every day? Yes, you will be doing all of these things daily. Now, do you do these things with immense conscious efforts? Do you always consciously plan out how you will be eating each item on your plate in sequence? Do you always check the phone log and follow the same procedure to call someone all the time? Do you always make sure that you pick up the brush and the toothpaste in the same order and manner every day? Do you check the GPS every time you go to your workplace? All of these actions seem absurd. I wonder who would be so harsh on their life and think so consciously about such small actions and thoughts. Yes, multiple things need conscious effort, but if we concentrate so much on such trivial things, we won't do the things that matter.

The human mind is very involved in itself. It is a classic conservationist and is always trying to use its finite resources most efficiently. If you were to get into your mind and see how it works, you would know that it lacks energy resources. As we discussed in the previous chapters, the mind has a finite store of energy, and it has to cater to thousands of thoughts every day. It has to process them and store them properly, which is not an easy task. Therefore, the mind came up with some energy-saving hacks.

The first hack that the mind came up with was only to do the necessary things. The storage and energy were limited, so the only task that the mind decided to do was process the information. It did not get into the troubles of segregating everything into 'the good' or 'the bad'; it merely left that work for the conscious side to do.

The next thing that the mind came up with was

something like a low-energy bulb! This thing was fascinating because this hack of the mind shapes how we live our lives. This energy-saving trick defines how we act, how we speak, and how we think about different things. The revolutionary hack that the mind came up with was: automation of actions— in other words— the formation of habits.

This revolutionary ability of our mind reorganized and changed our lives forever. Our habits determine our life.

So, what exactly are habits, and why are they so important? Well, habits are actions that you perform almost every day or at regular intervals.

What is so special about them? We repeat them so often that they eventually become automatic. When we are in similar circumstances where we did something in the past, we automatically produce the same action. We call this a habit. Such behaviors are compelling and have the capability of changing a person's life.

Do you still remember the questions that I asked you at the starting of this chapter? Now we can understand why thinking consciously about those actions seems absurd. You may have started brushing your teeth regularly many years ago, and by maintaining that procedure, you repeated it so many times that the behavior became automatic. Therefore you did not need to think twice before picking up the toothbrush or the toothpaste first.

You eat food all your life, which is why the mind has made that process a habit by automating it. You do not need to think about what to eat first because you will automatically just start eating however you like as soon as the food is in front of you.

When you travel to your office or school, you don't check the GPS all the time because, with enough repetition, your mind has become familiar with the route, and that is why it automates the directions in your mind, not making you think twice before making a right or a left turn.

When you call someone over the phone, you don't consciously try to put in the same procedure you think you should follow to call someone because you have done it so often that you don't need to think about the action again. You look up the person's contact on your phone and press the call button without thinking twice if this is the right way.

The mind does this when something occurs repeatedly; it makes it a habit. A habit is just the automation of specific actions or behaviors because you repeat them many times. When similar circumstances arise, the behaviors or actions take place with almost no thought or hesitation.

16

How are Habits Formed?

*"The law of harvest is to reap
more than you sow. Sow an
act, and you reap a habit. Sow
a habit and you reap a
character. Sow a character
and you reap a destiny."*

—*James Allen*

The mind uses habits to save a lot of energy by forming automated behaviors and actions. Without automatic behaviors, our minds would start analyzing and planning on trivial and very unimportant things like which shoe to tie first, whether to eat the noodles first or drink the soup first, whether to go out because it is a sunny day or stay inside because the sun may get blocked by clouds and it may rain. Whatever it is, concentrating on such trivial things and spending most of our time on them would have made it very difficult for us to do the important things that mattered to us.

But the big question is— How do habits get formed in the first place? It is an exciting process, and in this chapter, we will be diving into just that.

The first thing that the mind does to form habits is to note the various actions you do. The mind is an excellent note-taker and notes down even the most insignificant and small steps that you tend to forget consciously. As discussed in part three, the mind does not classify or segregate anything; it merely notes it down and stores it all. When the mind takes note of that specific thing, it tries to look for an opportunity to build a habit out of that action if it repeats.

For instance, a new doughnut shop has opened near your house, and you decide to go try that out. You like those doughnuts, and you revisit regularly. The mind notes the repetition of this action, and when it does, it will try to look for a specific pattern in your efforts to make them a habit.

We can use the mind's note-making process to our advantage and let it help us achieve our goals. How so? We can do it by deliberately doing the planned actions repeatedly and then making the mind note them down to form a habit out of them. We will soon take these actions without any friction or resistance because we will develop a natural inclination towards habit formation.

But, before turning our actions into habits, we need to understand the process of habit formation so that when we modify our actions into deliberate habits, we do it the right way.

As mentioned previously, the mind is always looking for new habits, as it has to reduce the amount of energy that it uses to do things. However, it just can't consider any behavior to be a habit. There is a set pattern for habit formation, which, when fulfilled, will make the habit stick. This pattern is known as the Habit Loop. It is known as the habit loop because the action or the habit continuously revolves in it, and the four-part pattern eventually becomes a loop that is repeated over and over without conscious effort. The four-part pattern or the habit loop is: -

1. ***Trigger.*** The first part of the habit loop is the trigger. When are you more likely to stop at a gas station to refill your car while traveling— when the fuel tank is near full or when it is near empty? The obvious answer is when it is near empty. Why do you do so? It is because the near-empty fuel sign is a trigger that warns you about being stranded. Therefore, you simply go ahead and refill your car. If there were no trigger like that, then you would stop at almost every other gas station to refill and would worry incessantly about the fuel going out. Imagine that the already burdened mind drives a car without a fuel sign, continuously worrying about the fuel going out. Do you then think it will be able

to handle thousands of thoughts and the stress caused by the dilemma of buying or not buying fuel? No, it won't be able to take the pressure, and everything will go haphazard. Imagine how calmer the mind would be if a trigger warned it when the fuel was about to run out.

It is the same with the habits your mind has created to reduce energy consumption. If there were no trigger present to tell the mind which behavior it needs to initiate, it would get confused with regards to initiating a habit or not. Instead of conserving its energy resource, it would have depleted it unnecessarily. Therefore, the first thing needed to form a habit is an empty fuel sign or a trigger.

2. ***Desire.*** The second thing in the habit loop is desire. When you do something, if it is not enjoyable or important, your mind will not do that thing. Therefore, when there is a trigger, there should be a desire for something after that; only then will a habit be registered in the mind's depository. When you see the trigger of an empty fuel sign, there is a desire in you— the desire to reach your destination safely without getting stranded. Therefore, you start to think about what to do to refuel. One of the most common habits, unhealthy eating, also originates from here. The trigger

for unhealthy eating can be various things. It can either be a visual image of a crisps packet, the aroma of a tasty doughnut, or the sizzling of a barbeque. Whatever the trigger is, there is a desire to eat that thing. Why does the desire come up? Because you want to eat tasty food that satisfies your gustatory senses and allows you pleasure. The trigger triggers a desire that pushes you further to take action.

3. ***Action.*** The most crucial part of the habit loop is real action, which happens in this step. So, the trigger causes a desire to arise, and to fulfill that desire, you go ahead and take some action. Very simple. So, if you desire to reach home safely and the trigger has told you that there is little fuel left, you will take the action of looking for a fuel station. As soon as you find one, you will go straight in and get your car refilled. All of the actions that you take are a part of this third step. Now, why do you take these actions? Quite simply, to fulfill the desire.

4. ***Result.*** The result is the last piece of the habit loop. The trigger made you desire something and the desire made you take some actions to achieve some results. When you reach the result, you fulfill the habit loop, and the mind notes this. Let's

say that you get your car refilled, and now you are good to go for the rest of your journey back home. In this habit loop of refilling your car, the result or desire is fulfilled by the knowledge that you will be able to reach your home after the refill safely. Now, the mind notes this pattern and stores it in the following manner, "When the fuel is low, trigger the desire for reaching to the destination safely without getting stranded, perform the action of refilling and fulfill the result of knowing that the problem is solved."

The habit loop works this way. When you repeat the action continually, this loop becomes a part of your mind and you. Therefore, the mind instantaneously creates the desire as soon as the trigger is 'activated.' Then the desire makes you take some action to achieve a result, and the habit loop gets fulfilled again. With repetition and practice, a particular action's habit loop becomes so automatic that you start taking the steps as soon as the trigger is provided, without even knowing and analyzing your actions with conscious effort.

Habits form this way. When the mind has multiple habit loops created, it does not need to use a lot of energy to analyze the action and situation. It quickly uses the installed habit loop to trigger automatic actions without giving in a lot of effort.

With this understanding, we can now proceed further and understand how habits can help us achieve our goals.

17

How can Habits Help us Achieve our Goals?

"Successful people aren't born that way. They become successful by establishing the habit of doing things unsuccessful people don't like to do."

—Willian Makepeace Thackeray

You may be wondering, all this habit stuff is fine, but how does it help in achieving goals? In this chapter, we are going to answer this question. To begin with, I want you to take this little self-assessment and answer the questions given below in "yes" or "no." Ready? Let's go!

1. Have you ever tried to learn something new and grow your skill-set?

2. Have you followed a lively and goal-aligned routine for yourself?

3. Are you consistent with your actions towards your goals?

4. Are you disciplined and dedicated to your goal?

5. Do you feel that you have enough time?

6. Are you able to finish everything you plan for in a day?

7. Do you avoid wasting your time on unnecessary activities?

8. Do you think you use your time well?

9. Do you have the right habits to achieve your goal?

Had a go? Great! Now, how many of your answers were yes, and how many of them were no? Tally them. Here is a simple result for you to consider. The more answers you have as "Yes," the better your habits and alignment towards your goal are. If you have more answers as "No," you need to align yourself with your goal.

Do you think all of the things listed in the questions above are necessary to achieve your goal and live a meaningful life? Yes, they are. And how many of these things do you think are affected by habits and small, consistent actions? Almost all of them are.

To learn something new and stick to it, you need to have the habit of accepting new ideas and not giving up on them too early.

To form a positive and goal-aligned routine for yourself, you need to build strong daily habits that help you take out the maximum time possible for working towards your goal.

Consistency, dedication, and discipline also come with strong daily habits that push you to work towards your goal.

When you have good habits in place, wisely choosing the triggers will help you find enough time in your day to work towards your goal.

When you form a strong routine with strong habits, you will be able to finish everything on your To-do list for the day.

With a robust routine backed up by powerful habits, you won't feel the need to spend time on unnecessary activities.

And finally, you will use your time well when you have good habits, and you will know that you have the right habits when every answer to those questions is "Yes"!

That's the importance of habits in achieving your goals. When you have the right practices in place, it becomes effortless for you to take the right actions, form the proper routines, and do it all consistently. Let's understand the importance of it through this example.

Suppose you want to become a computer programmer and you have invested in some courses. You start going through the various courses, and the long lines of code and technical jargon make you feel bored. You eventually think that this thing is not for you, and you quit. You quit because you did not have any supportive habits to support your learning experience and help you find happiness, thrill, and joy even in boring things like lines and lines of code. If you genuinely want to succeed at becoming a programmer, you need these skills, and if you quit, you will have to give up on what you want to do. Robust habits genuinely come into play here, and in the next few chapters, we will discuss how to form these strong habits.

18

The Story of Bad Habits

*"The chains of habit are too
weak to be felt until they are
too strong to be broken."*

—Samuel Johnson

As we discussed in the previous chapters, we need to develop healthy habits to achieve our goals and live a meaningful life. But before all of that, we need to understand how to get rid of the unproductive habits surrounding us. In this chapter, we will be discussing how to do that.

Humans have been walking on earth for the past seven million years. Still, the most drastic changes in our society and behaviors came only in the last ten-thousand years with the Agricultural Revolution. For the 6,990,000 years of human history, we behaved the same way, lived the same way, and acted the same way. However, somewhere about 10,000 years ago, we made the most drastic change and settled down to cultivate crops and grow our food instead of foraging it. Our lifestyle, society, and behavior changed radically.

Nonetheless, the mindset that we had developed in the 6,990,000 years of our existence did not change within an instant and is still with us today.

Imagine that you are traversing the plains of the African Savanna on a warm, sunny evening, still unsure of what was going to be your meal for the night. Another tribe member signaled that there was a blueberry vineyard about a hundred meters down the valley. However, there was another one across a mountain that had much tastier blueberries. You did not know if the vineyard existed across the hill, but you could somewhat see the vineyard a hundred meters down the valley. So, the most logical choice for you would be to go down to the nearest vineyard and munch on some blueberries, even if it meant that the quality was mediocre.

However, through the years, our thinking has developed, and our outlook towards life has changed a lot. We don't need to worry about the next meal because we have everything planned in our life. But this primitive mindset of going towards the thing that is the most rewarding 'right now' is still with us. Our world has progressed and changed radically, but our mindset still carries with itself snippets of the past.

Going for the most rewarding thing in the present is known as instant gratification. This one trait is the only major obstacle that we face in developing good habits. Let's simply understand this.

Our primitive ancestors were dependent on this trait for their survival because if they did not take what was right there in front of them and decided to wait until they got the best, they would not have survived. Why? Because they would have ignored what is already good to get the best, which they may not have been able to find. Instant gratification has been a vital survival instinct for most of human existence.

But as normal behavior, it is more unnecessary and harmful for us. In today's world, we see so many examples of the times when instant gratification takes the lead and gives momentary pleasure but long-term problems. If you eat a pizza every other day for one week, it won't affect your health or body shape. But if you continue this habit for months, there will be some noticeable weight gain. If you continue it for years and eat unhealthily every week, you will end up compounding a lot of fat inside your body, and you will become very overweight.

If you watch one more episode of your favorite Netflix series tonight, it won't affect your time management, health, or sleep. But if you continue to do it repeatedly for multiple nights, you will suffer from sleep disorders, lack of time management, and inadequate health because you will sleep late, wake up late, and do many things late in your life.

If instant gratification and immediate rewards are not beneficial for us, why do we chase them, and why do we go towards them? In the chapter about habit formation, we understood that some rewarding results follow the action to complete the habit loop. And, all the instantly gratifying things offer us pleasure and rewards right after we do them. The mind makes a note of this behavior or action. Now, we are more likely to repeat this action because there was an immediate reward. The cycle begins, and the more we repeat this behavior, the more the mind notes it down until the trigger, desire, action, and result are well-defined, and it becomes a habit.

Almost every person who has a bad habit will say that it started casually. Many alcohol addicts say that this habit of theirs often started as casual social drinking and then turned into an addiction. Many people who smoke say that they just tried it out for once, they liked it, and then they just did it again and again, until it also became a habit and an addiction. Many people obsessed with watching late-night movies often started this habit with their college roommates on Sundays and then carried it on by watching some TV till late almost every night. Most people who eat unhealthy food and are overweight started by eating junk food on an occasional basis, and then they just continued it.

That's the problem with instant gratification. When you choose to do something pleasurable in the present, you tend to care less about its future impact until that thing becomes a habit and changes your life. We choose instant gratification, and therefore we don't find true happiness that comes from giving dedication, hard work, and commitment towards a meaningful goal in life.

We don't choose positive and precious habits because they provide abundant rewards but are pain-staking in the present. Whenever we decide to do something that is not pleasurable in the present, like exercise, the primitive part of our mindset asks us to give up and take one more hour of sleep or one extra slice of a pizza. We don't take up the pain-staking task of exercising because it is not fast rewarding and does not fulfill the habit loop, where a rewarding result is required.

Bad, unproductive, and weak habits form in you just because you chose instant gratification. Remember, all the bad habits are instantly rewarding but painful in the long-term, just like choosing to eat in the mediocre blueberry vineyard a hundred meters away. Thus, selecting the instantly gratifying things will only give you mediocrity. All the good habits are painful in the present but abundantly rewarding in the future, like the top-quality blueberry vineyard across the mountain. It will take effort and persistence for you to cross the hill, but the reward of excellence and greatness will be truly worth all of that pain. Now, you choose what you want.

19

Choosing to Change the Bad Habits

If you want to achieve your goals, choosing the blueberries in the valley won't lead you to success, but picking the blueberries across the mountain will. To do that, you need to build excellent and robust habits that may not be rewarding in the present but will surely give you abundance and success in the future. The first step in this is getting rid of the bad habits that you already have.

James Clear has rightly said, "The outcomes in your life are the lagging measure of your habits-there are no high-performance people, only high-performance habits." This statement is the ultimate truth. Your habits indeed are the lagging measure of your life, and by seeing your current habits, you can predict your future. Your habits define you, and you need to make sure that they align with who you want to become.

If there are some habits that you need to change, then you must change them. If these bad habits hinder achieving your goal and the progress you want to make as a person, you need to change them. In this chapter, we will be focusing on how to eradicate the bad habits you don't want, because only after that we will be able to instill new and powerful habits in ourselves.

Finding out these negative habits is essential for you because you will not be able to understand what you need to change without this knowledge. One of the best ways to find that out is by observing your days keenly and picking out the habits behind the actions you take every day.

Mike was a young student studying in one of the top colleges in America. He was working as a part-time salesman in a local grocery store to earn some income. Mike gained a lot of weight; he did not submit his college assignments on time and was mostly late to work. His employer, as well as his teachers, were not happy with him. Being one of the brightest students in college, none of the teachers expected Mike to perform this poorly. Mike had the habit of not eating dinner but picking up a few things off the shelves in the store and eating them on his way to the hostel. After that, he would relax, watch some television and sleep around twelve or one at night. Mike woke up around seven in the morning, drank a cup of coffee, and then went to college to study. In the evening, around six o'clock, Mike's shift would start, and he would work till ten. This daily pattern was his routine.

When his teachers and employer spoke directly to him regarding his poor performance, Mike realized something was wrong and decided to change. The first thing he did was deconstructing his habit loops. When he looked at his day, he found that many unnoticeable yet negative habits impacted his day. He discerned his habit of eating unhealthy food and decided to change it. How did he do that? Let's see.

So, he started by looking at what preceded his habit of buying food off the shelves and what action succeeded it. He would often look at the clock during his shift to find out how much time was left, and he mostly saw the clock around 9:50 PM. Around this time, it was fully dark, and very few customers were coming in. The lack of customers and the time instructed Mike that it was time to go back home. These two factors also acted as a trigger for his desire to have dinner, and therefore to fulfill that desire, he took the action of buying the food off the shelves and eating it while going back home. These actions completed his habit loop by giving him tasty food to eat and fulfill his desire. This behavior was immediately gratifying, and as it got repeated on every day of his shift, it became his habit.

So, what did he do to change it? He used one of the most straightforward rules for habit change, and that is: keep the same trigger, keep the same desire, change the action, and try to achieve the result. Mike decided to set up a reminder on his smartphone for 9:50 PM, which said, "Buy veggies on the way home for dinner." Every time Mike accessed the same desire through the same triggers, he tried inserting a new action by reminding himself to buy vegetables. He now headed over to the vegetable section and often purchased some off the shelf. Next, Mike followed the same routine of going back from the store, but instead of eating in the car, he drove straight to his hostel, and before switching on the television, headed to his small kitchen and prepared dinner for himself. He watched recipes on YouTube and tried making them. After spending about an hour or so, making his hearty meal, Mike would patiently eat it and go to bed right away.

By changing one small habit, there was a change in another routine of Mike's, and that was watching the television. He now spent his entertainment time cooking, and by twelve, he was so tired that he did not want to watch any show and directly went to bed. By changing his dinner a little, his diet improved, and so did his sleep. He slept profoundly and woke up with energy. In the morning, he often had some left-over dinner from the last night, and he would eat that as breakfast instead of only drinking a cup of coffee. He felt more energetic at college and started getting back on track. He worked more actively in the store and followed his new routine of deliberately cooking healthy dinner in his kitchen. By changing his habit of eating unhealthily, Mike completely changed the way he lived his life. The first rule of habit change is: ***keep the same trigger, keep the same desire, adjust the action, and try to achieve the same result.***

By changing a single habit, Mike was able to change many different routines that impacted his life. One single habit of buying vegetables instead of junk food completely changed the way Mike lived. The habit that has a significant impact on other habits in a person's life is a keystone habit. In Mike's case, it was dinner.

Often used in ecology, the term "Keystone species" refers to a species that profoundly affects other organisms' lives. If these species were to go extinct, then other organisms would be affected negatively. In the same manner, if a keystone habit in your life changes, then other habits are likely to change. When you analyze your day and look out for habits you may need to change, you should look for keystone habits.

How? When you analyze a habit, you should imagine a scenario where you don't take that action or perform that habit. Suppose the consecutive actions change in the hypothetical scenario. In that case, the practice you are looking at is a keystone habit, and changing it will likely alter other habits that follow suit.

Isabella was another person who showed how strong the willpower to change can be. She was a young 24-year-old girl who dreamed of becoming a national level swimmer. When she was practicing one day, she lost control because some water entered her goggles, and she went straight to the pool's bottom. The security personnel picked her up after some time, but by then, she was unconscious.

The doctors at the hospital found out that the water had entered her lungs, and she had developed a severe infection. She couldn't swim anymore as she risked contracting the infection again if her chest and face were exposed underwater. She felt her hopes getting crushed right in front of her eyes. After her discharge from the hospital, she felt despaired, not knowing what to do with her life.

To deal with the stress, she started to smoke a little. She felt better after a smoke as it relaxed her for some time, and soon, she began to practice it repeatedly. She knew that smoking was bad for her health, but it soon became an addiction, and she did not go a single day without smoking at least one cigarette.

Her situation worsened, and after four years of

smoking continually, she developed a peculiar cough. This time she realized that it was different than a normal cough. Therefore, she went to the doctor, who gave her some heart-breaking news. He told her that she will develop chronic emphysema if she doesn't quit smoking right now. She was shocked. She did not want to spend the rest of her life coughing and sneezing with pain and shortness of breath. She decided then and there that she was going to change.

When she got back home that day, she collected all the cigarette packs she had and threw them in the trash. She deleted her contacts at the tobacco shop and changed her usual office routine because she was unwilling to let a disease get her to lose a great job she had come by after a lot of struggle. Whenever she crossed a tobacco shop and felt the urge to buy just one more cigarette, she would quickly turn herself and go to the other side of the market. After over four months of practicing this, her mind discarded the notes it had made for her habit of smoking cigarettes as she did not allow the triggers to come up anymore; there wasn't any action. She used the second rule of habit change to change her life and quit smoking: ***make the triggers as invisible as possible, the habits will soon move out of your life.***

However, Isabella did not do all of it with just one habit change rule; she used two! Whenever she met her friends at the bar or in a restaurant, they often asked her if she wanted to have a cigarette, and she would say, "No thanks, I am trying to quit." But even after saying this, she would feel attracted to take at least one smoke, and she did not know why she felt that way, even after telling her friends that she was trying to quit. She would simply walk away from her friends in such situations and often felt bad for letting them down. Then, she learned something about identity and self-identification. She was intrigued and tried to implement it the next time she was having a get-together with her friends.

Once again, the friends asked her if she wanted to have a cigarette, and she said, "No, thanks, I am not a smoker." After she said that, her friends too stopped asking her if she wanted a smoke as often as before. She did feel the urge to smoke the first time she said that, but controlled it, and soon she never felt the desire to have a cigarette even when she was in front of people who were smoking.

Doesn't it seem intriguing? How could one statement make such a big difference to a person's life? Well, all Isabella did was adopt a new identity. Let's break this down.

When Isabella said that she was trying to quit, she internally told herself that she was still a smoker and was trying to reduce her cigarette consumption. But deep down, she still identified with being a smoker, which is why she felt the urge. However, when she detached herself from this identity and decided to tell herself that she was not a smoker, it made a lot of difference, and she identified herself as a non-smoker. Thus she gradually stopped feeling the urge to smoke. She had completely removed all of her identification as a smoker and changed her life completely. The third rule is: ***make your new behavior/habit an identity to become a part of you and grow with you.***

These are the three ways in which you can change your bad habits and turn them into good ones. The first thing you need to do is deconstruct the habit loop and find the right triggers, right desires, and the right results. Often, the overlying action gives off the first impression to fulfill one type of desire, but we are continually seeking something else through that. For example, many people in an office take a four o'clock break to have a cup of coffee and some snacks, even when they just had lunch at 1:30 or 2 PM. The reason behind this eating is often not the fulfillment of hunger because they have already done it. It is usually for the satisfaction of socialization with colleagues, which happens over a coffee table with a few snacks on it! This way, you need to identify the underlying desires of your actions as well.

Identify your habit loop, understand what you

need to change, change it accordingly, and you will overcome all of your bad habits! It is only up to you to take action!

20

Introducing Positive Habits

"Humans are creatures of habit. If you quit when things get tough, it gets that much easier to quit the next time. On the other hand, if you force yourself to push through it, the grit grows in you."

—Travis Bradberry

Knowing how to eradicate bad habits is integrally crucial in paving your path to success. However, without positive and robust habits, you won't take concrete actions and succeed. In this chapter, we will be looking at the various ways in which you can build strong habits to improve your internal systems to achieve your goals.

The good, strong, and positive habits are the ones that offer immediate pain and late rewards. However, the habit loop completes only when there is a trigger, a desire, an action, and a rewarding result. Then how can we develop these habits if they don't have any immediate reward?

Well, that's a valid point. How can we build them?

Don't lose your hope as of now! There is a way out of this dilemma! If you look keenly, we say that these habits don't "have" an immediate reward.

However, nothing stops us from choosing the best way to induce these healthy habits into our lives— making our rewards for them! This method is one of the simplest ways to inculcate all the habit formation steps and create healthy habits that help us achieve our goals.

Let's say that you want to develop the habit of exercising daily. Nothing is rewarding in this habit because your body will pain in the first week, and it won't have changed much. You will also have to put in consistent hard work, and only then will you get the results. Therefore, building this habit based on future results will be difficult.

To make this habit a part of your routine, you need to put aside a reward for it. For example, you can say, "If I complete one hour of walk and fifteen minutes of yoga today morning, I will watch one more episode of my favorite web-series. And if I miss one work-out, I will cut down one episode for that day and not watch it." That's a pretty fair statement as you are giving yourself an immediate reward that you can anticipate, and this will complete the habit loop, which will allow you to develop this habit further.

However, only deciding on a reward is not enough because there are other things that you also need to do to make yourself stick to the good habits you want to induce. The different things that you need to do are:

1. ***Make the habit as easy and visible as possible.*** Being the first step in habit inculcation, this is also the most important. You need to make access to your new habit as easy and visible as possible because the human mind always picks up the triggers from its surroundings. When you surround yourself with the stimuli of your good habits as much as possible, the more likely you are to perform it. This way, you are reducing the friction between you and the practice, and therefore you are getting attached successfully.

   Let's understand this with the example of getting more fit that we discussed above. You have the goal of getting your body in shape to increase your capabilities of doing things and fulfilling your meaning. One of the best ways to be as healthy as possible is to exercise correctly and maintain a healthy diet. The exercise part of your health, as we know, can include walking, and the diet can consist of replacing chips and other junk food with fruits and nuts.

So, the night before you go to bed, you should set up your walking clothes, the shoes, the socks, and the tracking gear—all of it ready in a place that you see as soon as you wake up. This setup will act as a trigger and will make your mind anticipate the reward of the web-series. You will go for a walk because there is almost no friction for changing into your workout clothes and gear. Then, you need to set up your yoga mat in an open space in your house before leaving for the walk so that you cannot skip the yoga session as well.

Instead of keeping crisps on the kitchen counter, always keep two apples, a plate, and a knife, so that whenever you go there for a snack, you see a fruit that you can immediately cut. This way, you need to make your triggers as easy as possible to access and make the process of transitioning into them almost effortless.

2. ***Habit Towering.*** Just like books are put over each other to make a tower, you need to arrange your habits to create a Habit tower in your day, which will help you to organize or sandwich your good habits in a sequence and thus, you will not be confused about what to do when. You will have all the timings with you, and this will also make the transition from one habit to another easier. For example, if you want to

lose weight by going for a walk and eating healthily, you should write down and make a habit tower of your daily actions by starting at the bottom and going towards the upper part with the progress of the day.

You can state each of your habits this way. "First, I will wake up, refresh myself, change into my workout gear, go outside my house, and take an hour-long walk." This statement is one of the simplest examples of building a habit tower by stacking one habit over the other. You can create a habit tower in any way that suits you best, and you will have a plan of how you want your habits to play out every day. This sequence will give your mind a pattern to recognize, and it can also take a previous practice as a trigger for the next one, and it can work as a chain reaction. It is up to you how you decide to use it.

3. ***Make it your identity.*** We discussed this in the previous chapter and talked about how Isabella got over her habit of smoking. Whenever you are trying to build a new habit, you must make it a part of yourself and your identity. When something becomes a part of you, it combines with your existence, and therefore you must use positive statements and affirm

that you are already what you wish to be through the habit you are trying to develop. If you continue with the example above and say that you want to lose weight by walking and doing yoga, you can say and affirm to yourself in the present tense that your habit is a part of your identity. For this example, you will say it this way, "I am a fit and healthy person. I am an early riser. I walk, and I do yoga every day as my health matters to me." Statements like these will help you make your goal a part of your identity, and you will soon be able to achieve it.

4. ***Declare it publicly.*** This technique is one of the most unique and effective that you can use to achieve your goals. We usually think that we should keep our goals to ourselves and show them to the world once we have achieved them. However, publicly declaring your goal can make you achieve it better! Confused? Don't worry, you will understand. So, when you declare your goal out publicly, your pride and your self-image get involved. Let's continue with the same example of losing weight. You declare it to your family and friends that you will go for a walk and do yoga every day and lose 80 pounds in the coming 12 months. When you do this, your pride and your image of yourself in other

people's eyes is in question because if you fail to achieve your goal or build your new habit, you will fail in front of other people, and they will always look for opportunities to poke or mock you on that basis. Nobody likes that, and to save your pride, you will try your hundred percent to go for a walk no matter whatever excuse you may be able to come up with, and therefore you will stick to the habit.

You can inculcate many different habits this way to achieve your goals! Initially, when you consciously perform a routine consistently, you are often doing it for the sake of the reward. But with enough repetition and automation, the habit will become more about the process than the secondary reward.

Why so? Because you are not forming the habit of achieving the side reward, you are developing the habit of achieving your goal. So, when you decide to build a habit, you need to concentrate on *who* you want to "become" instead of *what* reward you want to "get."

If you only incessantly think about finishing the task at hand to achieve the reward, you won't form a habit that sticks because you are not giving your attention to what you are 'doing' in the present but to what you will get soon.

Remember, you will truly develop a habit and make it stick when you focus more on the process and keep the rewards just to finish the habit loop.

Try your best, reward yourself, consciously control the habit loop, and you will be able to control how you take actions and how your life turns out!

21

The End…?

"Celebrate what you have accomplished, but raise the bar a little higher every time you succeed."

—Mia Hamm

You now have all the tools in your hand to develop the right habits to help you take action and achieve your goals. Getting rid of bad habits and trying to stick to good habits no matter what is one of the most challenging tasks, but not impossible. All you need is excellent dedication, determination, and consistency. When you have all of this with self-belief, the right plan, and the right passion, you will truly shine when you achieve your goal!!!

But, what after achieving it? You may ask. Do your dedicatedly formed habits, plans, and passion go away after you have reached your goals? Will the habits that you developed from scratch and worked on for a long time simply end? Will all your efforts die when you achieve your goal?

These kinds of questions may daunt many people because the thought of losing all of your hard work, persistence, and consistency with one achievement is genuinely disheartening. What will happen to all of your habits when you reach your goal? Let's find out.

First of all, I would like to clarify that a goal is *not* the end of passion, purpose, and meaning in life. And therefore, it is *not* the end of the habits you have built with so much consistency. It is also *not* the end of the self-belief and confidence you have developed. Why so? Because a goal is a one-time achievement. After you achieve it, it is over, but life is not. Life continues to prosper, and so do the habits, meaning, and self-belief.

When you develop your habits and self-belief, you are not only creating them for the sake of a goal; you are making them for life. That is why strong habits and self-belief don't end with a goal. They continue to grow and prosper because you develop internal systems that support you for life in the process. A habit forms the system and method that takes you to a goal and stays with you for your life until you decide to change it.

It means that the meaning, passion, and purpose also go on after achieving the goal; but how? Let's understand that!

After achieving the goals you had set for yourself, your life won't end there. By achieving a goal, you have only unlocked a certain percentage more of the potential you have inside yourself, which means that you have expanded the number of things you can do in your life by achieving a specific goal.

Let me give you an example- Imagine that you always loved reading fictional books and were very good at storytelling. You wrote many short stories and shared them with your close friends, who always loved them. You felt that you should write a novel as you were good at making stories, and you loved reading them yourself. The thought of writing a book seemed very daunting to you. You thought to yourself, "I am good at writing short stories of probably 2-3 pages but writing a 200-page book isn't possible for me at all!" You shared this idea gloomily with your friends, who in turn encouraged you to take this chance. You started.

You wrote a beginning like you usually do. You started adding many more dialogues and descriptions in your writing. You set out about 30-40 minutes a day for writing your novel, and you just kept writing about half a page every day. You did this continually, and after about 400 days, your book of 200 pages was ready! You got it edited, you got it checked and read by your friends, and you published it. Your book got great attention and appreciation from people, and you felt delighted due to this appreciation. You felt genuine gratitude towards your friends who supported your idea in the first place, and you owe your success to their support. After this, you know that you have pushed your limit of capabilities further, and you have expanded your potential of doing things. You have indeed achieved greatness in your life, but then, a question arises in your mind— "What now?".

To answer the "What now?", you need to look into yourself. Remember, you have only expanded your potential fractionally with your goal, not entirely. So, the answer is to make new goals, achieve new things, and further expand your potential. You need to keep learning and keep the excitement burning all the time in your life. Your age can never decide when you can or cannot learn because no matter how old or young you are, learning will be omnipresent all the time.

Grow in your passion by making new goals, learning new things, and achieving excellence in all that you do. You just need to keep setting the bar higher and higher and keep learning more and more. Let's look deeper into this by continuing with the example above- You have written a book, and it has achieved great success. What do you do now? Well, if it interests you, write another book. Maybe a sequel to your first one or a new story altogether. But you will want to do this because you will want to go back to the spotlight again, you will want to be appreciated again, and you will want to be grateful again, but this time on an exponentially higher level!

Always strive for learning, growth, happiness, and fulfillment. No matter how much you have already achieved, learn more, and achieve more. Also, even if the world doesn't see or appreciate your success, if you know that you have grown exponentially, then you truly have. Dwelling, dreaming, and living on the appreciation you get once for achieving your goals won't take you to greatness in life, but continuously and regularly keeping excitement and achievement a part of your life will bring in the excellence you seek. Your efforts for finding meaning, purpose, and happiness will genuinely create a significant difference in your life because, after all, your growth is your responsibility.

CONCLUSION

First of all, I would like to congratulate you on reaching the end of this book!!!! I hope that this book helped you find your passion, set goals the right way, believe in yourself, and form new and strong habits. Now, I would like you to use all the knowledge you have learned from this book and implement it to help a friend. When we implement our knowledge and grow through it, we can truly understand it. Consider this book as a math book. To understand something that you are confused about, you don't need to reread all of it—well, if you want, you can do that—but you can directly visit the chapter that you need to understand again, and that will be a great way to brush up all of your learnings and knowledge.

Now, let's put all of your knowledge to the test and see how well you can use it to help a friend. But, wait! Don't just go out looking for a friend who needs help deciding what they want to do in life or what they want to change.

You can even help our made-up friend here—Jim! A few years ago, he lived in Miami, but his company offered him the chance to double his salary and move to the Dallas branch. He agreed to do that, and soon, he left Miami and ended up in Dallas with his family. His neighborhood and society had changed entirely. Everything was fine, but one problem emerged. In Miami, Jim had the habit of going to his local gym daily and exercising, but this habit dropped in Dallas. First, there was the fatigue of shifting, and then he had to get into his work as soon as possible. He was working a little late to earn even more and get another promotion very quickly, and that is why he started eating at multiple fast-food joints he crossed while going back home. This behavior resulted in unhealthy eating, and Jim began gaining weight.

After two years, he felt that he had changed a lot and that even after working overtime and trying to do as much work as quickly as possible, he hadn't got any promotion. His health diminished, and his relationship with his family developed conflicts as he rarely ate at home and didn't spend time with his loved ones. He felt that he was in complete turmoil and wanted to change. He did not feel fulfilled and meaningful in his work anymore and thought he was not good enough to get a promotion. His self-belief started going down, and now he comes to you for help.

It is your time to give him the advice with the things you learned. Now, when you know about all that Jim did in Miami and all that he does in Dallas, you can compare and understand where the root cause, the main mistake is, and now you need to think over this to give Jim the advice you think will work.

My most straightforward advice would be, "Go to the gym every day and stop working over-time. Instead of that, produce much more qualitative work in the office hours and then spend the evening with your family on the dinner table."

Why would I advise Jim to go to the gym if I were his friend? Keeping fit and having confidence in himself gives him the energy to go and excel in other fields. When he went to the gym while in Miami, he felt as if he had started his day with power, and that helped him make sure that he was giving in quality work, which then got him the promotion. Now, he was not going to the gym, and ate unhealthily because he could not feel confident and became ignorant. In other aspects of his life, this was true as well, and only because of bringing one change he could trigger another good change

Now, it is your time to apply your knowledge of habits and beliefs to help Jim bring in transformative results in his life by taking action. Get to work and use your understanding now!

Had a try? Great. If I were to give Jim some advice on doing this, I would tell him to use the principles I have discussed in this book and ask him to do the following things. First of all, I will ask him to understand why he wants to change his current behaviors. We must know *what* we want to change and *why* we want to change it.

Achieving this clarity is one of the most critical steps in understanding how to set the right goals.

Once he knows why he wants to change, I will tell him to make a goal for himself and make a statement out of it in a precise manner. Next, I will ask him to keep that goal in mind and then buy a gym membership or hire a personal trainer. The next habit that he will need to develop is stopping his work at four in the evening and then driving back home to his family. Habit stacking or towering plays a significant role as he builds new habits by taking the right actions.

Now, it is time to help him get over his inferiority complex and make him self-confident and self-believing the same way he was in Miami. To do that, he needs to find out why he feels doubtful and inferior about himself. Then he will work to bring about improvements in himself and get over his fear of not being good enough for anyone by breaking down his misconceptions and forming new beliefs.

Now, when Jim implements all of this and brings back the habits that made him successful in Miami, he will be able to come out of his negative beliefs, live more healthily, and do qualitative work. All of these actions will get him the promotion he long-awaited!

You can implement this book in your life this way. Even if there was one new thing that you gained from this book, I would be humbled, and I would have fulfilled my purpose of helping people fulfill and achieve their goals! After reading this, I hope that you are ready to take charge of your life and become happier, successful, and more fulfilled. I express my deepest gratitude to you for reading this book till the very end because your presence as a reader is what fulfills my purpose and makes me worthy of being called an author.

On a parting note, I would like to conclude this book by saying that your life is your ship, and you are the captain. You start to navigate this ship into a vast ocean from the time you are born, and as you continue into life, you advance your ship into the sea. Now, you have control of your ship, and you have the choice to do whatever you want to do with it. If you're going to let it sink, you can do that, but if you're going to lead it to the most beautiful coastline in the world where all of your long efforts will pay off, you can do that as well. By implementing this book, you choose to give meaning and purpose to your life and decide to go to the beautiful coast. By squandering away your time meaninglessly, you will allow your ship to sink, and that is how it will all end, without any purpose, reward, or meaning. Both of these are choices you have, and both cease at death— the only difference is that one gives you happiness and a feeling of being light and truly satisfied. In contrast, the other gives you lifelong regrets and no satisfaction, leaving you with a heavy heart longing to live again.

Now, it is up to you, because in the end, you are the captain, and you choose what happens with your ship.

Thank you!

ACKNOWLEDGEMENTS

Expressing my thoughts to the whole world has been my dream, and this book has brought it to reality. Writing a book has been a completely different experience for me than reading one! Creating this book and putting my knowledge into precise words would not have been possible if I did not have the support of these people around me:

1. First, a big, big, big THANK YOU to the Universe for allowing me the opportunity to fulfill my purpose and become the medium to pass this knowledge out to the world!

2. I would express my deepest gratitude to my source of creation, my mother, who gave in hours and hours of hard work to read my manuscripts multiple times and suggest improvements and additions that helped me enhance this book's content exponentially! Thank you, Mom!

3. My dad has been the second supporting pillar for me. I am deeply thankful for all of his cooperation and efforts to help me in whichever way possible! He always ensured that I had and got everything in time to make my journey frictionless! Thank you so much, Dad!

4. A big thanks to my brother, Virgyanpreet, who aided me every step of the way, allowing me to get my head around technical things and the cover design process. His little yet powerful celebrations on every small milestone brought a smile on my face and positivity every time!

5. My aunt Baljinder has been a constant source of support and motivation for me! She always gave in her encouraging suggestions with love and kindness, for which I am forever grateful!

6. I am eternally thankful to all my loving family members, my aunts, uncles, and cousins, who always wish the best for me!

7. A special thanks to my aunt Sheetal for her constant appreciation and motivation for every piece of my writing! Her innovative ideas sowed the foundational seed of the idea behind this cover! And to my brother Piyush whose dedication and creative thinking inspired me and the idea behind this book's cover!

8. I will be forever indebted to my excellent teachers, who taught me essential life skills and enabled me to possess various qualities that shape my personality today! I am grateful to my teachers because they taught me how to spread my message by

showing me the infinitely vast sky that depicted the range of my abilities!

9. Even though I could express and write my thoughts on the paper, this book would have remained mediocre, unclear, and unfulfilling if my editor and sister, Gauri Kolhe, had not polished my work to excellence. She gave her best to bring this book out in a direct, clean, and concise manner! I am eternally grateful to her!

10. They say, "Don't judge a book by its cover." But often, the best-bought books are the ones with a great cover! I am incredibly thankful to my cover designer, Ranjit Jose, who brought this book's concept to life by designing a phenomenal cover! I sincerely appreciate his cooperative and proactive efforts that made this book come across in such a lively manner! Thank you so much!

11. I would like to thank my mentor and coach, Som Bathla, who gave me the hope and the path to become an author and publish this book with full freedom! Without his consistent efforts to continuously help me grow, I would not have gained so much knowledge and fulfill my purpose of writing this book! Thank you so much!

12. And finally, I would like to express my deepest good wishes to every person on this planet, because I know for sure that their presence has to create a meaningful impact on this beautiful world! And that includes you, too :)

FURTHER READING:

What Books Inspired the Author:

1. Atomic Habits By James Clear.

2. The Power of Habit by Charles Duhigg.

3. Man's Search for Meaning by Viktor Frankl.

4. The Almanack of Naval Ravikant by Eric Jorgenson.

5. Think and Grow Rich by Napoleon Hill.

6. Attitude is Everything by Jeff Keller.

7. The Alchemist by Paulo Coelho.

8. Unlimited Power by Anthony Robbins.

9. The Calling by Priya Kumar.

ABOUT THE AUTHOR

If you are an avid reader, you have probably read this section with the beginning, "Hello! My name is............." That's boring! I am not going to start that way because you probably read my name on the cover, and by reading the introduction, you would have gotten a pretty fair idea of the inspiration and the source of this book.

I am going to start with who I am on a personal level. If you are a fun, light-hearted, happy, curious, fulfilled, calm, and well-directed person, we are friends because I am just these things! Being an author in the personal development and self-help genre, I believe that the names already contain the primary truth. This genre is known as "self-help" because what you are doing is helping yourself, and therefore in your life, I am nothing but the guide or the escort showing you the path to meaning, success, and fulfillment. It is up to you to decide if you want to walk the path or not! With this book, I am giving you the key to meaning and happiness, but it is up to you to decide if you want to open the lock with it or not.

But, I don't just end here for you. I must inspire you to take action. I must inspire you to change your life to the way you want it to be, and then it is up to you to leverage on that inspiration. As an author, this is who I am for you. If I can fulfill that purpose, I matter to you, and that is what I aim to do! This book is more about you than me, and therefore I have tried my best to give you enriching content to the fullest to achieve success in life. Only then will I become the author, the inspirer, and the gateway for you. If you fulfill your purpose, only then I come into existence for you!

I hope that after reading this book, you feel that I have become the author, the inspirer, and the gateway for you! If so, then I would love to connect with you and understand how my book could impact your life because a reader creates an author, and I would like to be the one you cherish!

You can connect with me in the following ways:

On my website prabhsimratgill.com

My email: prabhsimrat@prabhsimratgill.com

My Social Media Handles:

Instagram: prabhsimrat.gill

Twitter: @PrabhsimratG

Facebook page: Prabhsimrat Gill